MW01046819

The Advent of a New Hope

By

Dr. Lilian I. Asomugha, PD., DNM

authorHOUSE™

1663 LIBERTY DRIVE, SUITE 200
BLOOMINGTON, INDIANA 47403
(800) 839-8640
WWW.AUTHORHOUSE.COM

First published by AuthorHouse 06/03/05

ISBN: 1-4184-9386-4 (sc)

Printed in the United States of America
Bloomington, Indiana

This book is printed on acid-free paper.

ACKNOWLEDGMENTS

****

I will not fail to give my hearty thanks to all those who have helped me to write and bring this book out to the public. I have been encouraged by several good people in all that I have done. My first acknowledgment would be to the people who gave me the first and greatest encouragements of my life, my parents. I want to thank you, Mama and Papa, for being who you are to me. For the education you gave me and for standing by me, especially during childhood years, when I needed you most. I thank you, Mama for all your motherly prayers and advice. I thank you for always reminding me that God had not finished with me and that He would never forsake me.

To my four children, Chisaraokwu, Chijioke, Nnamdi, and Udodirim. I want to thank all of you for your support and encouragement. Your characters and behaviors are what spurred me into writing this book. If you did not accept my moral teachings, I would not have any reason to write this book. I am proud of you all and pray that nothing will separate any of you from the love of God our Heavenly Father. Thank you for making me proud and I thank God for giving me you.

To all my brothers and sister, Mrs. Joyce Okeneme. I thank you all for your relentless support, prayers, cares, and concerns.

To all my Christian brothers and sisters from my church, I say thank you. I give special thanks to our women's ministry, prayer ministry, the golden agers prayer group, my pastors, and all those who prayed for me.

I must say my hearty thank you to friends and relatives, Mrs. Eunice Sampson and all the good people who stood out for me and supported me in my time of distress. You all prayed for me, visited me, and comforted me. May God bless you all, one by one.

To some of my employees, both past and present, especially Mrs. Shelby Chance, who understood my pains and worries and stood by me when I needed help. To those people that I have met and interacted with, whether friends or family, you have all encouraged me when you call me blessed. Even to those who despised me, your challenges gave me reasons to ignite my praying powers. Because of all of you, I am able to write this book in appreciation of your support.

To my friend, Mrs. Mary Obasi who answered to my passion and joined me in founding the Nmadinobi (Beauty is in the heart) Women Association. A support group for the needy.

Finally, my greatest acknowledgment must go for my Maker. The one who authored my life and from whom I draw my strength, God Almighty. To Him be glory and honor through Jesus Christ my Savior.

TABLE OF CONTENTS

INTRODUCTION

The world we live in is like a marketplace. All kinds of things are bought and sold in this market. You can only sell what you have, and what you buy is your choice. Because the world turns in circles, we must be careful not to end up buying what we had already sold.

We require wisdom, which does not come by chance. We ask for it and it only comes from God through Christ our Savior. Two things are obvious about our existence here and these are that we are created to either live or die. The word of God tells us in the book of **Deuteronomy 30:19.**

…..That I, God have set before you life and death, blessing and cursing: therefore choose life, that both thou and thy seed may live. When we choose and buy with wisdom, we have loved and obeyed God. He will then bless us with the joy of everlasting life.

This book is written with the purpose to remind most people that there is time for everything in life, and there is reason for every encounter. God knows and sees everything about us. We have no reason to be discouraged or lose hope or faith in God during our life's storms.

It is a collection of my personal encounters, prayers, passion and a reflection of God's promises to you and me, as it is manifested in the Bible. We have a reason to be here on earth, and while we race through this earthly journey, we will come across so many ups and downs. We must not be discouraged.

To my friends and family, those who call me blessed, those who wonder and ponder over God's goodness, and to those who I may yet meet in my walk of life, I wish to say to you that the road is never short or straight. It's rough, rugged, long, and lonesome, but through having strong hope in life and my faith in God, it is counted all joy. **When you read this book, you are taking a journey with me. In this**

journey, you will find that I was not alone. I was never alone and will never be alone. I had problems, I made mistakes, I cried in my distress, but I called on my Heavenly Father day and night. He said that He would never leave me nor forsake me.

The Advent of a New Hope is written to help the many men and women all over this world who are facing any kind of adversities to understand the will of God for them, His Children. The statement, **"It could have been worse"** should be a powerful force to help us ignite our praying powers, knowing that God is always there waiting and watching for us not to stumble. If not for God's sake, His grace and His love, life could have been worse. The statement further tells us of the Amazing Grace of our Heavenly Father. He is the only one that can make things better.

Sometimes it may not be your choice that you will be doing the things you do, or that you will encounter. At some point in one's life, things happen that can drastically change the way the person lives his or her life or maybe the way one looks at life itself. Whether it is your making or not, when life's storm hits your door, your best choice is to do whatever you can to survive the storm. That is to say that you need to overcome such storms. The only way to do so will be to look up to God and hear His voice. Negative or unacceptable events in our lives are not necessarily designed to destroy us. Things do happen to strengthen us when we are about to slumber in faith. Since the way we look at life reflects how we live it, it is my advice that we should start looking at life with a positive attitude. You must build a strong foundation by having faith in our Lord Jesus Christ. When the storm of life hits, your faith would guide you to keep focused on Christ and you will not sink in that storm.

Our faith in Christ strengthens our hope, and in turn, leads us to the fulfillment of our purpose in life. No matter what may come your way, learn to take it to the Lord in prayer. If it turns out good, take it to the Lord in prayer of thanksgiving. If it does not meet your delight, take it to Him in prayer for deliverance. The bottom line is that we will always give Him glory regardless.

I want my readers to look at my experiences and those of others as shown in this book as a reflection in their own lives. The stories you are about to read are based on true-life encounters. May this book serve as a source of motivation, providing spiritual and emotional support to uplift you and help you understand that God is always there for you and is only a prayer away from saving you.

PART ONE

CHAPTER ONE

How Did You Do It?

The key words here as we read this book are these three essential tenets of life: **Purpose, Faith, and Hope.** According to the dictionary, **purpose** is defined as "intention" and **hope** is to desire with the expectation to fulfill or accomplish. In hope, there is complete trust and reliance. **Faith** also is complete trust and reliance. We look at the Bible definition of faith as it is in the book of **Hebrews 11:1. Faith is the substance of things hoped for and the evidence of things not seen.** Therefore, we must know that for those who have hope, life must have purpose that must be fulfilled. By the same token, for those who have purpose for life, there must be hope or the desire to fulfill that purpose. Our hope for life and our purpose for life all lie in the hands of our faith in God through Christ. This is evident that our complete trust and reliance is what carries us through in our earthly journey. When life became too strange and seemed unbearable, by faith I asked God what He wanted me to do, what was His purpose for me in life. My hope was built on whatever He would reveal to me. It was rough but with time, I have counted it all joy.

When life seems fair and beautiful, we must be grateful for that fairness and beauty. We should never prize anything more highly that the value of each day. Our lifestyle gives us our value for each day we see. When you wake up on a given day, you realize that you had briefly forgotten the troubles of this world. You had a good dream and a sound sleep. You had gone to an unknown world of peace. You are well rested. That is to assume that you had a peaceful night. As you opened your eyes, you could still perceive the fairness and beauty of life. Around and about you, your body tells you that everything is well and everyone is fine. **What would you do?** Whatever your conscience may tell you, just remember, that "life so fair and beautiful" should not be taken for granted. It is then time to say gratitude and praise to your Maker.

Each day that we see is a given grace from God. It is a favor that we did not deserve because of our sinful nature, but God allows us to see each day as He wills. Sometime, someday in life, one might wake up and sense that something strange had taken place around him or her. Something has changed. Things are no longer looking the way they used to. You see yourself helpless. It might have been a gradual or sudden change. It could have been a spiritual, mental, or physical change affecting you directly or indirectly. You realize that "Life is no longer fair and beautiful."

What do you do? Whatever your conscience may tell you, just remember, that "Life is no longer fair and beautiful" should not be taken for granted. It is then time to say gratitude and praise to your Maker.

What I am trying to say here is that no situation in life should ever be overlooked. In every situation, we must turn things over to God, our Maker. He knows everything that is beyond our understanding.

My personal view of the world we live in is that it is a huge marketplace. We all run helter-skelter, buying and bagging. Everyone wants a full bag. Nothing is being discarded. No one is ever satisfied. Have you ever stopped to look at what you have bought? Have you stopped to check if you have bought wisely? Did you consult the chief merchant, the owner of the market on how best to shop in His market? You may not have control of everything about you in your life, but your shopping bag is your responsibility. It is what you are ready to take home from the market. If someone would ask, how did you do it or how did you shop, what would you answer? Did you take anything for granted?

In order to shop right or survive the market strategies, we need help from the expert owner and never take anything for granted. God is in charge and in control. If we depend on Him through Christ His son, we will never go wrong.

I have always been asked the question, "How did you do it? How did you survive? How did you raise such wonderful children?" As a young couple, my husband and I never knew how to answer those questions. We always looked at each other and smiled whenever someone asked. After he passed away, I still encountered the same questions. I was not able to answer these questions because sadly enough, I had taken things for granted. I could not count my blessings nor see God's hands on me. It was not out of ignorance. It was only because of the same sickness that has swallowed us up in this world, "taking things for granted."

Tragically, I became a single parent when it was least expected. I had given up the hope of continuing the good work my husband and I were doing together. I was convinced that I was not going to be able to continue that good work alone, but for some reason, I am still encountering those same questions, "How did you do it? How did you survive? Do you know you are blessed? How did you do it with your children?" Of course I did not know how. I never thought of how; I had taken it for granted or maybe I had concluded that that was how it was meant to be. A teacher once asked me the same question when my youngest child came to her elementary school to join the kindergarten class. My older three children had been in the same school. I looked at her, not knowing what to say, and she answered her own question, saying, "God did it for you, you have such wonderful children." I simply said to her, "You are right." Most Christians like me take things for granted. We believe in God yet we fail to realize how good He is to us. We fail to give Him honor for what He has done in our lives.

These questions and more have followed me all my life. Friends and family and even strangers have all asked me these questions. Once they come to know my family, the question follows. I sit back to look at my life more now as a widow, and I know that God has a purpose for my life, and because of that, He has led me through in every trial and tribulation. It was unimaginable to me when I suddenly became a widow. Death does not ring a bell at the door or announce that it is coming but under certain circumstances, even Christians would ask, "Could God not make exceptions in this case or at least warn us, be careful, I am about to do something." If He knows everything that happens to us and can stop us from hurt and pain, He could at least say, "Child, I love you, I will warn you before time."

The truth is that God does not wish us evil. Several things we blame God for or label Him with are not His making. He has given us everything we need on this earth. He has planned our lives long before we were even born. We will not know these things until we take a closer walk with Him through Christ our Savior. If I knew then what I know now, I would have had no reason to doubt His power, what He has done for me, or what He was about to do for me.

At the time of my distress, I failed to realize that God has a major role to play in the lives of every man and woman on the surface of this earth. It does not matter what you think or do, God has charge over everything about you. Whatever problems you may be facing on earth, He knew it long before you faced it. All our difficulties and even all our joys are well known to God. Satan may come in any form to separate us from the love of our Heavenly Father. But if we believe and put our faith in God, we always will have victory. Having hope in the one and only God, who knows all our life's purpose, is the only way we can overcome all the problems that we encounter daily as we live. At any time in our lives, we need to know that God is watching out for our well-being and that there is nothing we can do to help ourselves on earth except by His grace. We must stay close and in touch with our Maker to understand His will for us. He made us and therefore the purpose of our lives is His.

God created man in His image and commanded us to worship Him. In addition to worshiping Him, He has a specific duty for each and every one of us here on earth. The fulfillment of that duty that He has set aside for you is your choice. The desires of our hearts to be free from problems, to be happy, to be saved, and to have eternal life becomes our responsibility. We will not attain this freedom unless we turn to God and do what He has called us to do.

Following my husband's death, it took me several months to even years to actually realize that God is in control of my life. When I began to understand His ways more than I ever did before, things started to look different for the better. Saying that I am a Christian was not enough to carry me through my ordeal. As I came in close contact with my Maker, life became a lot fairer and brighter.

CHAPTER TWO

When Tragedy Hits Our Door

Allow your hope to rest fully in God's hand in order for Him to fully fulfill your heart's desires in your life. The storms of life do not discriminate. We must pass through one kind of storm or the other before we make it through or out of this world. You must be prepared and be strong to withstand your storm when it comes. A strong foundation of faith and your focus on Christ will pull you through in any storm.

Some of the characters in this book have been changed to fictitious names for identification purposes. My personal experiences and the fact that I am able to overcome most of those heartbreaking, painful moments is part of what has prompted me to write this book. It will not be fair on my part to live the rest of my life without letting other people, all the men and women out there in the world who are suffering silently and ignorantly, know that God is powerful. He is mighty in every battle. He is great and will fight every war for those who have faith in Him. It is amazing what God can do. It is not a secret what God can do. Do you remember the song that says, "What He has done for others; He will do for you"? If so, What He has done for all other believers, He will also do for you if you believe. For those who are wondering, is God still there? Does He still love me? Can He see what I am going through? Does He know about it? When is He going to help me? As you recount all these in your mind, remember that any good things that you desire in life can only be a reality if you have hope in Him. You should not forget that our hope in God is the expectation that He will fulfill our desires which is to free us from the bondage of adversities of this life. **"Delight thyself also in the Lord, and he shall give you the desires of your heart." Psalms 37:4**

If we should make God our utmost delight, He will fulfill all that we hope for, all that we long for, and all that we desire. To have hope in God and to believe that He will surely fulfill our needs is to have faith in Him, which means that we must then have complete trust, loyalty, and obedience in Him. These are the things God requires of us. God wants us to have complete trust in Him. He wants us to have strong faith in Him. He wants us to have deep respect for Him. If we do all these, there is no question then where our hope and expectations would lead us to. Our hope in Christ starts when we totally and completely surrender our lives to him. That is to say that when we show our respect to God by building our hope in Christ, the (solid rock), and surrendering all our needs to Him, our desires will be fulfilled. I will always remember my favorite song of hope and trust:

> **My hope is built on nothing less**
> **Than Jesus blood and righteousness**
> **I dare not trust my sweetest frame**
> **But wholly lean on Jesus name**
> **Chorus: On Christ the solid rock I stand all other ground**
> **Is sinking sand all other ground is sinking sand.**

It is obvious now that we know whom to turn to when we need help. From this song, we know that all other ground is sinking sand. Unless you stand on Christ the solid rock, you are on sinking sand. Your foundation is not going to be strong for the great storm. The sinking sand has no hold of its own and will not support you. You probably would now be able to guess where I am coming from. When nothing seems right and friends or even family seem to have left you, when you feel like a rolling stone and your head seems like you are on a roller coaster; when night seems too long and days seem so short; when upon life's billows you are tempest-tossed; and life seems to have no meaning, no fun, and it seems like there is nothing to live for, then it is time to re-evaluate your relationship with Christ your solid Rock. Surrender your life and all you have to Him. Trust not in man, for man is nothing but sinking sand that has no hold of its own.

Remember the old saying that if those who killed Christ knew what it would have meant, they would not have killed him. Rightfully, this is a statement for every human being. We all joined hands to kill Christ. Was not the idea to stop Him from proclaiming His rightful heritage as the Son of God? Then what? After His blood was shed for us on the cross, for over two thousand years now, His Gospel must be preached in every corner of this earth. We could not wipe his name off of this earth. His life was already written before He came to this earth. He came to suffer and die for us that we may be saved. Is it not the same for every one of us? Our lives had already been written even before we were born. Yes, it is written, and whatsoever God has written, so be it. The devil has no power over any of God's children and cannot deprive us of God's love if we believe in God through Christ.

Only the blood of Jesus Christ will help you and save you in time of trouble. Tragedy may come at any time, anywhere, and anyhow. It is one of those life experiences that no one wants to welcome. We do not want it, but in one way or the other, sometime in one's life, unimaginable things sneak in only for the simple reason to challenge our relationship with God. Satan will always plant the seed of discord, but in every adversity, we must not forget that God is always in charge of our lives and will be there for His children. For Christians who already have relationship with God, overcoming the power of the devil in times of trouble may not be equally an easy ordeal. It is sometimes hard to withstand the pressure of adversities. It is necessary then to be strong in times like these. Yes, be strong and unless you are on a solid Rock, the sinking sand will devour you in just a short time. We must not fail to realize that we have not been promised a bed of roses, but even if we were, we should equally realize that roses grow between thorns. There will be thorns in our wonderful lives. Overcoming the thorns (the storms) of life is what makes us who we are.

For some people, the loss of a job is a tragedy. The loss of a loved one such as a friend could become an unbearable tragedy. The loss of property, investment or position, respect, etc. may be tragedy for some people. In this book, we will be looking at tragedy that hits right where it hurts: when a child loses a beloved parent or parents. When one loses a beloved spouse, when a strong member of the family, the mentor, the breadwinner, the focus of everyone in the family is lost, that is when it hurts, That is when life does not makes sense and we say life is not fair.

The death of my beloved husband seemed unbearable. I felt the torture of life's storm. I was angry with God and everyone around. I could not understand life's uncertainty or the ways of God. It was then hard to pray as before. It was difficult to comprehend that life or anything made sense anymore. I thought of withdrawing to solitude but could not because of my children. Through the help of good friends and God-fearing people, I was able to step out of my predicament with a positive attitude towards life. Since then, I have met with and spoken to several men and women, widows and widowers, divorcees, orphans and people with other forms of adversities. Regardless of what the situation may be, everyone shares in the agony and fear of rejection that comes after a tragedy.

Ours was always a happy home. Although my children are grown now, I still hear their little voices singing **"When**

daddy is in the family, happy happy home.. happy happy home happy happy home when daddy is in the family happy happy home happy happy home." We go on to, "When mommy is in the family, happy happy home..." and we go on till we have sung with everybody's name. Finally, "When everyone is in the family, happy happy home..."

We had a happy home. Needless to recount how happy that evening was, a Saturday (Sabbath) evening when he came home from a long trip to Nigeria. All seemed well and everyone was very happy as he talked about his trip. God, in His infinite mercy, did not give us any clue as to what His plans were for all of us. Yes, God really moves in a mysterious way His wonders to perform. Little did we know that as we all went to bed, one of us was not going to see the next morning. We prayed and thought that everything was in order before going to bed. The children were fine and no one complained of any ills. About two hours after we went to bed, I was awakened by a loud, deep breath. I tapped my husband to wake him up and instead, he gave out a louder, longer, deeper breath. In fear, I jumped out and across the bed to his side. I shouted out his name, felt and pushed him. I screamed at what I saw. My high-pitched squeaky voice sent a flashing alarm all over the house.

And as I screamed to God for help, my children were running into our bedroom. Seconds later, my oldest child was calling the ambulance as I tried giving my husband CPR. My three younger children were at the foot of the bed, rubbing Daddy's legs and praying as I told them. When they asked what was wrong, between giving CPR and trying not to frighten them, I heard myself saying, "Daddy is leaving us, he is not dying, just keep praying." I was so scared that I did not know what I was even answering the children. I believe that I was scared more than they were. I tried to act strong and comport myself. It seemed to me like I was trying the impossible. As the ambulance arrived, I had a moment of relief, hoping that these paramedics would do something that I could not do. I was praying and asking God to spare my husband's life. It was the most horrendous night in my life.

As I watched the paramedics working on my husband, my mind raced through so many thoughts. I could remember when one of them asked me to leave the room. The look on his face was so uncomfortable. You could see the frustration on his face when he could not get a favorable response. He felt even worse when I said to him not to worry about me because I understand what was going on and that I am in the medical profession. I watched my husband as he lay motionless in the ambulance. My eyes switched back and forth between his motionless body and the faces of the paramedics. As if they were trained not to show any emotions, I could not get anything out of them. I tried to fight tears, although I knew that crying was not going to help anything. I prayed all the way. Shortly after we arrived at the hospital, he was pronounced dead. Did you think I believed the physician? I looked up as if in search of God's face and screamed in the language I speak best, saying, "Chinekem, Onye nwem ahapukwala nanim n'ebea," meaning "My God, my Lord, don't you leave me here by myself." I kept on repeating those words like nothing else could save me at that moment. I wanted God to hear me and do something better. The physician had walked towards me saying, "And he was very young." I said in response, asking, "He was?" His countenance was full of grief as he spoke to me. It was the worst moment in my life. It was nothing but a mistaken dream to me.

It could not be true. I refused to accept it. My sister arrived just in time to rescue me. I remember telling my sister to go and check if the physician was lying to me. Seeing the tears rolling down her eyes confirmed the unbearable. I felt tightening in my stomach, my hands and feet were numb, and my throat immediately felt completely dried. I could no longer cry. My head was heavy and I trembled. Shortly after, my pastor and his wife arrived. Another family friend arrived with his wife. It was now obvious to me that yes, I am alone. The pain was even worse when we came home to my children and one of them asked, " How is Daddy?" Our problem was how to tell them that Daddy was no more. When nobody spoke, another one asked, "Did daddy die?" Someone answered, "Yes." Everyone started crying.

From this moment, nothing would make sense to me anymore. All I could think of was that life has changed for my family. Something must be done. God must do something to make things better. He could still perform His miracle and send someone to come and say that it was a mistake, he did not die. I could not think right any more. The autopsy revealed that he had a massive heart attack. Several days passed and even weeks, and our house was always flooded with people. Friends and family came to show their support for our family and their last respect for our hero. My husband was honorably laid to rest in our native land, in eastern Nigeria.

If we know why things happen the way they do, we probably will have reason to accept several things without questions. It was not easy for me to accept that I had become a widow in the twinkle of an eye. It did not make sense to me and I know that it was not going to make sense any time, any way. How could my children suddenly become orphans? Why wouldn't their father live to see them grow up to be adults? What happened to our faith in God? If only I could scream out my anger to God and ask Him my questions, I would do so without hesitation. At this time, I was not ready to lay my burden at His feet. I was just going to let Him know how disappointed I was. I was going to ask Him why He could not see that we needed Him to save my husband's life. I was going to ask Him about all those promises He made to us. Lord, what about long life? What about good health? What about the joy of a complete family, happy, happy home? What did I do to deserve such mishap? Every question I could ask God came to my mind. I could not find an answer to my questions. Life is just not fair. Nothing could stop my tears.

CHAPTER THREE

Why Me?

It has been a month now since he was laid to rest. The world seemed like it stood still for me. My life was in disarray. I felt like my whole life had changed forever. I was never going to be the same, and I was afraid that things would never be the same again. I could not imagine what this would mean for my family. I wondered if people really knew what I was going through. Of course, people knew my plight. Nonetheless, many did not understand nor would they ever understand what this meant for my children and me. This is the turning point in time of one's life (as a Christian), you must close your eyes to the world and focus on God for guidance and protection.

I did not do the right thing. I did not do what I just told you. I thought that I could handle everything or everyone that worked for me or against me by myself. One good thing I learned later was that regardless of what situation you may find yourself in or what situation people may subject you to, you need to be **true to yourself and be strong.** Some may come to your rescue while some—especially the ones you may least expect it from—will choose to disappoint you at this moment.

As time went by, I realized that I was living in denial, thinking that there might be a miracle. Fear overtook me and became my worst enemy. This is where our Christian faith comes to test. What would a Christian do in a time like this? This is the time we seek God and turn to Him for deliverance. I did not do it. This is one of the reasons why I am writing this book. It took me so long to let go. I first nagged and cried and blamed and wished all kinds. It was not right that my husband should die. How can I be left alone with four young children? My children were between ages of nine and sixteen years. The sixteen-year-old was just a few months from graduating from high school. She was ready for college and had already visited the university of her choice with her father. My sons were twelve- and thirteen-years-old. My baby was nine years old and she had always asked, "When is Daddy coming home?"

Daddy had gone on a one-month trip to Nigeria. It was very devastating for her when Daddy came home and did not make it till the next day. I was overtaken by worry. I had a strong feeling of anger toward God. I feared what would happen next. What other mystery will follow his death?

Coming from a country where every death, as in many third world countries, has some kind of mystery behind it, I was in fear of what was going to happen next. To some of us, a massive heart attack after a long trip was not enough and would never make much sense. Modern technology tells us what we believe these days, but for me, regardless of what anyone may think, I was angry enough to blame it on God. First of all, if He allowed this to happen, then it is well with me but why? Why could He not wait for later? If God did not allow it, then where was He? Why did He not stop it from happening?

There was the feeling of anger, loneliness, frustration, and even resentment. How can this happen to Christians or to a Christian family? God did not even consider the fact that my children needed their father. What did we do to deserve losing our father and husband? I put all the blame on God rather than bring all the complaints to Him. Although we still prayed every morning and night, my daily stress increased. In my inner most heart, I continued to ask the question, why me, Lord?

"Why me?" seems to be the most frequently asked question whenever something goes wrong. When our hopes have been shattered, we ask, why me? When we are disappointed, or there is an accident or death of a loved one, the first thought that comes to mind is why me? One thing we forget is that this question portrays a negative feeling. When we are looked down on or we did not get what we think we deserve, we wonder why it was not on someone else. From now on, I felt like "why me" has become my watchword. If God loved me or cared for me enough, He would not let me suffer this loss at this time. Have you ever had any reason to think that it should not have been you? Have you ever had a reason to ask God why it has to happen to you? If so, you may closely relate to my situation. If you can think of how many times in your life you have had to think "why me," you can then imagine how many times you have thought evil against someone else without knowing it. After all, you did not name anyone.

Several months passed by and I could not see why it was me. Day by day, and slowly and slowly, my negative emotions grew stronger, and my questions remained unanswered. I found out that no one could answer this particular question. I started to ask myself if I really was looking for an answer. I wondered how I would feel if I heard the true answer to my question. I know that I needed to hear something and that thing would be the answer that I very much hope will satisfy my curiosity. We do ourselves more harm than good when we hold onto negative feeling and refuse to understand that every will is of God and that there is nothing that happens to us in any day that He is not aware of. God, of course, does not wish His children evil. When tragedy comes, we cannot say that it is God's will, but we know that He is aware of it and aware of our feelings. Our hope is that He would take care of these things to free us from pain or hurt. We need to ask questions but we must be careful of what we ask. "Why me?" is an incomplete question. It only exalts the person asking it. It looks down on the rest of the world. When we ask the question **why me,** we forget the other half, "Why not John or Mary?" The second half of this question equally triggers a feeling of anxiety and must be let out to help us either answer the first half or even answer the question fully. The negative feelings we embrace in our daily lives should help to strengthen us rather than make us weak. They are the storms of life. They will come and sometimes they come unexpectedly. To most people who will find themselves in this situation, passing through the storms of life, I want you to know that the earlier you realize that negative feelings and questions have no answer to your problems, the sooner you will put those burdens down and move on with your life. Lay your burdens down at the feet of our Lord, Jesus Christ and things will be better for you. Do not wait too long.

When we start asking negative questions after a tragedy, just like I did, we open up room for doubt in our lives. All the ifs such as "if only" and all the whys **"why me,** are never going to make anything better. These questions bring undesirable feelings. They leave you with a feeling of abandonment, emptiness, and void of love. They equally leave you with anger, hate, loneliness, and rejection. Despite the goodness of some people around me, I still wanted to know why it had happen to me. No one is perfect enough to divert misfortune to other people. If we would think of it, we will very well agree that there is no reason to allow these negative feelings to steal away God's love from us. How then can we know not to worry when things that are beyond our understanding happen to us? How can we know the will of God when we lose a loved one? Does it even make sense to think about His will at this point in time? What good will God have for you when He could have stopped the tragedy and let you just be happy as a Christian? The truth is that God did not stop it. He knew about it and He wants you to grow from that experience. Do not be afraid to ask or receive answers from God. I surely forgot that God is still in charge. He still wants me to recognize that and glorify Him for the tragedies I escaped. It could have been worse. He is a wonderful God. No matter what life has for you, be ready to glorify His name at all times. The Bible tells us that in everything we should give God glory. You may ask, "How can I give glory when I am in distress?" I asked the same question. I was told that it is our Father's command and we will obey it.

In Isaiah 24:15,
Wherefore glorify ye the Lord in the fires…..

No matter how difficult the situation may be, we must give God glory.

He will keep you in perfect peace if you keep your mind on Him and trust Him, says
Isaiah 26:3,

As a Christian and one who loves God, I knew not to ask questions, but to accept whatever comes my way, hoping and praying that God will make do for me, come what may. I prayed daily without ceasing. Although I trusted God and thought I had given Him my burden, I knew that down deep in my heart, I still felt like I had been spotted out and chosen for doom. I knew that I did not deserve this doom and I was not going to let it weigh me down. I started listening to my inner self. I started to pray differently. I asked God to help me to accept my situation as I have seen it. I delighted myself with the prayer of serenity. Asking God to reveal to me what He wanted me to know or do from this time on. Life has completely changed for me. How well can I accept this change? Is it really something I can handle, and if so, what difference would it make in my life?

I knew very well that I could not change the loss we had just experienced. I could only change the things that I understood. I needed wisdom to deal with everything that came my way. My biggest problem was about raising my children as a single parent.

I needed to gather up some courage so as not to disappoint my children. I tried my best to make them think that I was fine. It was only God and Him alone that knew what I was going through. I knew that my doubts and fears were all displayed in my physical expressions. Mentally and even spiritually, I knew that I needed the help that could only come from none other than God. Only by His grace and through the Holy Spirit in me could I be rescued from my distress. In my family, we prayed morning and evening routinely. Getting everybody together for prayer was not a problem for me. We were all in search of God's will and His answer to our questions. I did realize several months later that my fears were our fears together. Each one of my children held their peace just like I did. No one wanted to be the weakling. We must show courage, support, and unity in all that we do from now on. We shared the same anger, frustration, and disappointment while waiting for God to give us a clue as to why it had to be us. The feelings we shared brought us all closer to each other and to our Creator.

During evening prayers, we discussed our days, and one by one, we shared what happened to each one that day. Sometimes we would discuss a note or a card that someone had sent. Sympathy cards from people helped to make our days. A family friend had sent a card that said all the good things about my husband and added to it, "look at all the wonderful children God has given you to cheer you up, knowing that there will be a time like this." Uh, so God really knew beforehand?

Another card said that if my husband would say or see anything at this time, it would be that I should continue to walk in the light of God and take care of his family. Several people sympathized in their own way and each one was very encouraging. I was determined not to make any mistakes, and I asked God to take me in His hands.

One Saturday evening, I asked the children if we could make our devotion a special one and sing Daddy's song. They all agreed although they did not know which song I meant.

When my husband traveled to Nigeria, I had taught them a song in our native language (Igbo) and told them to sing it for Daddy in Igbo as a surprise welcome home song the day he comes back. They did not have the opportunity to sing this song to him. It was sung at his funeral.

They waited for me to choose the song. When I told them which song, they were all quiet for a moment. Someone asked why we had to sing that song. I had no answer for them except that I felt that we needed to sing that song in his honor. "Let us use it as a tribute to Daddy," I said. "Okay, that's fine," they said.

English	Igbo
How sweet the name of Jesus sounds	**Aha Jisus di ok'uto**
In a believer's ears	**Na nti onye kwere**
It soothes his sorrows, heals his wounds	**O nakasi ya n'ahuhu**
And drives away his fears	**N'achupu egwu ya.**
It makes the wounded spirit whole	**On'agwo oria nkpur'obi**
And calms the troubled breast	**N'ajuru'obi nsogbu**
'Tis manna to the hungry soul	**O bu nri nke onye agu**
And to the weary rest.	**N'enye izu ike.**

I knew that it was going to be difficult for us to sing that song. I was already battling with tears.

I knew not to show my emotions and I knew too that my children were very skeptical of my choice of song at this time. We sang the song. First we started like it was the worst thing we ever knew. We all looked at each other as if to say, "Did you hear what you sang?" I requested that we sing it again, and by the third time, we had picked up courage and sang it like Christ had given manna to our hungry souls. As we were singing, it felt like Daddy was there with us, saying how good the song was. We are accustomed to praying in turns. As we knelt down, I called on the child whose turn it was to pray. He was hesitant and sighed in dismay. I thought that perhaps he forgot that it was his turn on that day. I looked up at him and nodded my head. He did not acknowledge my gesture. Then I asked why? What's wrong? As I looked at him straight in the face, I could see the feeling of fear, anger, and doubt in his face. Suddenly everyone looked up. My children were all looking at me like I was crazy. I felt like I had done something terrible. All I could say was, *What?* He said, "Why do we have to pray anyway? After all these prayers, and I thought we were Christians, yet Daddy died." At this point, they all turned to me and said, "Yes, that's true. Why do we have to pray anyway? Why did he have to die?" I thought that I could seek help from my oldest child who was sixteen, but she looked at me and equally said "Yes, Mommy, answer his question." They asked to know why Daddy had to die. Don't we pray enough? Aren't we Christian enough?

I felt an urge to say something but could not. I wanted to go ahead and pray but I knew that the question that was asked needed to be answered first. I was going to answer it but I felt like there was some heaviness around my throat. As we gazed at each other, I picked up courage, and with a calm and steady voice, I said, **"We do not know why he died, only God knows why and unless we pray, we will never know the reason."**

There was a sigh of relief. We prayed, but before we dismissed to go to bed, I reminded them that God has a purpose for everyone on earth. When our work is done on earth, we must all go back to him. Daddy finished his work and had to go. I did not know what put those words in my mouth. I was as confused as my children, but believe you me, these were the very words that gave me courage in dealing with my situation. It was this particular prayer time that opened my eyes to see and know that we all shared the same feelings in our ordeal. My pains were not different from theirs. They loved their father as well. These children are also asking unspoken questions, "Why me." Where was God when it happened?

Through prayer, I realized that we needed each other. We had to be closer to one another and this happens best during prayer. At mealtime, we may find someone who says "I am not hungry and I don't want to eat." But during prayer, we come together anyway, whether or not we wanted it. Gradually, we realized the need to come together. No one wanted to be in his or her room when the rest of us were praying downstairs in the family room. It had been our tradition before now and it would continue. God reveals to us those things that ordinary eyes would not see, ordinary minds would not think, ordinary people would not feel, only if we are spiritually bonded with Him through prayer. You may ask me now how I survived or how I raised up four wonderful children. I will gladly answer that after wondering around in thought and lost in fear, God had mercy on me. I turned around to the things I knew but did not do. With faithful prayers, strong hope, and trust in God, I survived.

Amazingly, I realized that my answer to my son's question was just God's own words in answer to my own prayers. "We do not know, we can only find out through prayers." God answers prayers, sometimes even before we ask. He knows about the unspoken innermost doubts in my heart. **"Why me?"** He allowed me to answer my own questions by my responding to the spoken feelings of my children. I have been chosen to guide these children. How much doubt and uncertainty can I harbor in my heart? I needed an answer to my questions and it has been so answered. We must know that the answers to every prayer are never too far from the prayer itself.

Those many questions that pondered my heart each day needed to be answered. I knew that God would hear, so I relentlessly prayed, waiting for Him to reveal to me every thing that I needed to understand.

I asked God to teach me and reveal to me the thing that I need to do in order to know Him better, serve Him better and be closer to Him.

CHAPTER FOUR

Just A Faithful Prayer

In our daily lives, we find out that there are many obstacles, some of which we may not be aware of until they become too large. Sometimes these obstacles seem to look so easy to overcome that we take them for granted until they become overwhelming. When our problems become overbearing, we should not start wondering if God is still there or if He really cares. That is when a prayer is needed and just a little faithful prayer will carry you through.

We tend to complain more about things we see and can compare. Whereas the things we do not see and cannot even imagine why they interfere with our lives are truly the things we need to focus on. These things are the things that really bring us closer to God. Our feelings, our emotions, our expectations, and thoughts are the main things that define our relationship with our Maker. They are the things that we deal with in our daily lives. Our toils and tribulations are based on these things that we cannot see, and they govern us.

When life gets tough and things get rough, we blame God instead of taking refuge in Him. We need to know that God works diligently with us in times like these to make things better. Things may seem slow, and indeed it was slow for me. I thought that God was not fair and was not listening to my prayers. It was obvious to me that He probably would not answer my prayers. I thought that it did not make any sense, but each time I prayed, I felt some sort of hope or maybe some sense of security in me knowing that I prayed anyway. Come what may, God will one day answer my prayers. I always reminded Him that I was not supposed to be left alone. I needed Him to guide me. I knew that if I must survive this, it would only be by His grace.

Sometimes I would ask myself if I was really praying right. I remember crying out loud one day, asking God to teach me how to pray if He thought that I wasn't praying right. Why do I even have to pray when it seems like nothing changes? Some moments I would be fine and seemed to have great hopes and expectations, but the next moment I would be questioning and doubting again. Thinking about prayer, I realized that this is the only mystery between God and those He loves. It is the only way that I can communicate with Him. I cannot communicate with God through tears. God does not want me to lay my burden at His feet with doubt. He wants me to trust His ability and to look up to Him with faith. If He could not do it for me, no one else could. God knows our every weakness and all our problems. He knows my innermost thought. I cannot hide my feelings from God. Whether spoken or unspoken, He wants me to bring my requests to Him in prayer. Unless we learn to come to God in prayer, we will never have a closer walk with Him. In walking closely with Him, we will then understand His will for us. I could not understand His will until I realized how to faithfully lay my burden down at His feet in prayer.

Prayer is the soul's sincere desire,
Unuttered or expressed.
The motion of a hidden fire
That trembles in the breast.

The dictionary defines prayer as supplication or expression that is addressed to God. It is the sincere desire that burns in our heart. It may or may not be spoken, but only God knows the depth of it. We can only relate it to God in prayer. As I told my children that we could only find the will of God by praying without stopping, I realize that I was giving myself a duty that I must fulfill.

I was not going to sit back and tell them to pray and find things out by themselves. God put those words in my mouth to let me know too that I must find out for myself why certain things happen in our lives. Prayer became my weapon, and as I prayed each day, I became closer to God and to my children. I found peace that gave me the courage to hold onto life. I fell in love with the word of God more than every before. Some people saw me as a woman of great strength and courage, but I knew that I was very weak although prayerful as I hung on to God's promises.

The Bible—I call it God's love letter to man—became my strong support and guideline. I found so much comfort in doing things that I do, knowing that God loves me. After all, He made me for a purpose and I want to serve that purpose before I go back to Him.

Soon my children began to realize too that we must pray together in other to continue staying together. Every once in a while when it was time to pray, I will hear them say things like, **"a family that prays together stays together."** I chuckled with joy each time one of them said that. We know we needed each other and we were ready to be there for one another.

I am sure that many men and women who have been in this situation will agree with me that there are times when nothing made sense at all except when you come together as a family to share God's love in prayer. Sometimes I would think that things would be clear and smooth by the next day, but it did not happen. Rather, things would get strangely more difficult to understand. Where is God? Does he really want me to continue living in this condition and if so, how? I did not give up. I continued to pray for His will.

I thank God for my Christian friends and family. I had prayer partners, and my mother, who all joined hands to pray for my family. My church family was always there for us. It is amazing to know that in times like this, even children can be the best source of hope. As I was busy wondering how to be a single parent to my children, I found out that my children were busy wondering how to help Mom to cope with being a widow. My being a single parent was not a problem to my children. They just wanted to make sure that they would not be a problem in my life. They wondered if I would ever stop crying. One time, I had told them to be strong, trust in God, and do not cry, they looked at each other and almost in unison said, "Yes mom, but just don't be the one to start." Gradually I realized that they were even stronger or probably could handle the situation much better than I could.

I had quite a few favorite verses in the Bible. I found great comfort in these verses. It seemed like anytime I read these verses, I felt like God had given me the greatest lift, strength, and courage to carry on in life.

Psalms 5:1-3,
Give ear to my words, O Lord,
Consider my meditation.
Hearken unto the voice of my cry,
My King, and my God:
For unto thee will I pray.
My voice shalt thou hear in the morning,
O Lord, in the morning
Will I direct my prayer unto thee,
And will look up.

I read and sang these verses every day. I could not leave home without reading or singing this very psalm. I woke up every day with the song in my mouth. I loved it so much that I had to put it on my message phone. I wanted everyone who called my house to know that the Lord was with me and that I talk with Him every day. It was necessary for me to alert people and let them know that the Lord was my shield.

I promised myself that God would hear my voice every morning. I will direct my prayers to Him and I will look up. Not only did I pray or call upon God, I spoke to Him like He was there by my side. I directed my attention to Him. I looked up to Him and I told Him that I knew nowhere else to send my plea. At night, I spoke to Him quietly as I lay on my bed.

I started to list my prayers to God.

.....**Send your holy spirit to comfort us and teach us to love you with all our hearts.**

.....**Take away the fear in our hearts and guide us in all our relationships.**

.....**Give us life that we may not die and put our lives in the right order.**

.....**I want to live and see my children grow, so protect me from all my enemies.**

.....**Teach me that I may teach my children right and give me wisdom to make right decisions.**

I could go on and on to an endless list. Like a little child would ask a father, I started asking God to do these and more for me.

I am the fifth child of the twelve children born to my parents. I was told that three of these twelve children died in infancy. Nine of us grew up to adulthood. My parents were Christians of the Anglican (the Church of England) faith. All of us children grew up to embrace and accept the Christian faith. We were all aware of what was expected of us as Christians. We studied and read the Bible as we grew up. Talking to God in prayer was not new to me, yet I could not understand why it was hard for me to comprehend why certain things should be the way they are.

My husband was equally born in a Christian home. His father was one of the founders of the Adventist church in his village. After our marriage, I became an Adventist. We both loved God and our church. We have four wonderful children, what people call a perfect family of two sons and two daughters. We were well involved in church activities. We had no reason to doubt what God can do. I personally knew how wonderful God is. God had always been good to us. We are one happy family, and we know that He was never going to fail us. So where was He when tragedy knocked at our door? I could sit back now and ask myself how much I really knew the ways of God. Did I have any reason then to doubt that He would take care of things for me?

No, and it should not be strange if I should ask the same question my young son asked. I could ask it in a different way. Why does God let bad things happen to Christians? Is there any justification to such? Why would we suffer pain and loss, even when God knows very well that we trust Him? I know that there are many men and women, widows and widowers, divorcees or orphans and more who ponder over this same thought day and night. I found the answer to my question through prayer and supplications. By trusting, believing, and having faith in God, and not in any man, I realized how wonderful He is. I want us all to realize that no matter what may come your way, God is the answer. I am a living witness as to what God can do for you through prayer.

It is by the grace of God that everyone survives in all adversities. Our salvation is oftentimes within our reach but we overlook those things that remind us of our Maker or His love and care. It took several months and even years for me to realize these things. The prayers we read or say every day only make sense when we settle down to figure out what they mean and why we say them. When we say, "Thy will be done O Lord", do we really need His will? If we do, why then do we worry after praying?

When His will is done, why do we shy away from it. We must make sure that our prayer requests are what we need from God. He wants to work with us in the fulfillment of our desires; so when that time comes, we need to allow Him guide our steps. We need to sometimes look at some old-time prayers to help us know how to present our petition to God.

The Prayer of Serenity

This is a testimony that I can say was meant for me yet a prayer of hope and faith for all. I call it a perfect prayer made for me. It is a writing that gives a blessed assurance that our Lord, Jesus Christ is there for us, to help us comprehend the things that are beyond our understanding.

God grant me the serenity to accept the things I cannot change,

The courage to change the things I can;

And the wisdom to know the difference.

I had always read this prayer inscribed on a small plaque sitting on the entertainment center in our family room. It was just a prayer then. But when someone sent me a card with this prayer in it, I began to read a different meaning into it. Prayer is one of the many things we take for granted. If only I could accept the things I could not change. If only I could leave it up to God. If only I could understand that God does not want me to dwell on these things. If only I could understand. If I do, then I will ask Him to give me the courage to change what I could and teach me how to know what is good and what's not. It is just but a short prayer that tells it all.

At the moment I discovered the prayer of serenity, I realized the need for understanding God's will for me. I became aware of the fact that I needed courage and that I had no power or strength of my own to do anything in my life. I realized that I needed wisdom to do everything that I planned to do. It was important that I knew the differences between things that I choose to do and things that I had to do. Praying is my choice but praying faithfully is what is required of me. I made sure that I asked for wisdom in all my prayers and decernment for all my decisions. I asked God to take control of my life so that I will not walk with the ungodly.

Happiness is a necessary part of our daily life. It is a state of well-being and contentment. We strive for satisfaction in what we do. Happiness comes as a result of satisfaction. Finding joy or happiness in what we do is also part of our satisfaction. We happily have hope in God because we know the He will satisfy our needs. God satisfies us through our faithful prayers to Him. I wanted to be happy. I wanted satisfaction. I wanted to know that by trusting in God, I will once again have my happiness and satisfaction in what I do. I asked Him to bless my works and make me content with what I have. I prayed the prayer of Jabez several times.

The Prayer of Jabaz.

1 Chronicles 4:10

And Jabez called on God of Israel saying,

"Oh that you would bless me indeed, and enlarge my territory,

That your hand would be with me,

And that you would keep me from evil,

That I may not cause pain!"

I wanted to pray like Jabez. God granted him his request. He prayed with faith and trusted that God would hear him and fulfill for him. The more I read the prayer of Jabez, the more I thought of my faith in God. I thought that I was not faithful enough or trusting God enough to pray like Jabez. I wondered if my prayers were reaching God right. As I repeatedly read this prayer, I started to memorize it, and say it every time I prayed.

Every Christian should know this and be able to ask for God's promises with an open mind. If you believe in God through Jesus Christ His Son, you should not be ashamed to ask Him anything nor to claim His promises. The prayer of

Jabez was one of my favorite prayers in the Bible. I needed God's blessings in all things, so I picked up courage and asked for it. I needed Him to bless my business and I asked for it. I requested that He should take charge of everything about me and bless me indeed. I never stopped praying this prayer of Jabez. *Father,* I said, *bless me abundantly so that the world will know that your hands are on me.* I began to understand my own prayers. I knew what I needed, and I asked for it, just like Jabez. In seeing the light and finding my path through hope, I rededicated my business to God and renamed it **NEW HOPE PHARMACY**. My hope in Christ must be made manifest in everything about me, including my home, my family, and my business. **Proverbs 16:3,** Commit they works unto the Lrod and thy thoughts shall be established.

I asked God to bless me to love what I do, and to. establish my works to be blessings for others and to be glorifying to Him.

So many Christians these days would pray and tell God what it is not about instead of telling him what they need. When you pray such, you will get what you asked for. God surely hears prayers, so be careful what you pray for. A prayer of faith, prayed in confidence, trusting that God would not fail you is what He requires of us. I want you to know that prayers are answered. Although it may not be answered right away, do not lose hope. Continue to pray because the one who knows your heart's desire will give you what He deems best for you when it is due. This is not a preacher's statement. I am only a living witness to what God can do when we ask in faith. The prayer of Jabez is very interesting. I grabbed it like it was another one of God's special notes for me. He did not ask for simple blessing. He made sure that God knew the depth of his request. He said, "Bless me indeed, enlarge my territory." He asked for deliverance from evil and asked that he may not cause pain to anyone.

Isn't that amazing? We can see that he specifically asked for wealth, riches of land and money. He asked for deliverance (forgiveness) and pleaded that he may not sin.

I knew that I had no need for territorial blessings at this time, so I asked God to bless me and my children and everything that I would lay my hands on. When Jabez asked, he asked for what God would do for him and also what he wants God to help him do. Even as we ask for God's blessings, are we willing to stay away from evil? Do we ask God to help us stay away from evil? If so, do we ask with all our heart? Jabez asked for these things too. He knew that God requires certain things of him and so it is with all of us. I asked like he did and God heard my prayers.

We are told that his mother called him Jabez, saying, "Because I bore you in pain." Jabez asked that his hands may not cause pain. He understood the feeling and the agony of pain. He did not want pain on anyone else. When we go through pain, and we find ourselves in times like these, or when we have tasted pain regardless of what kind, we know not to wish someone else the same. We must then start praying like Jabez. We must start asking God to keep us from being a part of any kind of pain on others. Pray even for your enemies that they may be free from pain. Do not ask "**why me?**" It is a sin to cause others pain. When people cause you pain, take it to God in prayers. He knows best how to handle our enemies. Those who delight in the downfall or misfortune of others will surely have to answer to their wickedness. I resolved to faithful prayer and asking God with confidence.

The Footprint (my prayer of testimony and trust)

It makes my day till eternity whenever I think of the footprint. It makes me remember that my God is always able to carry me through. I know He is always with me. I know that I am not alone when I think of the footprint.

A dream of reality. The man in the footprint had his dream. It must have been comfortable for him as he walked through the storms of his life, knowing that his savior was on his side. He had no reason to fear. Suddenly, he realized that his help did not seem to be there anymore. Most of the time—especially at the saddest and lowest times of his life—the two sets of footprints had become one set. He was disturbed, afraid of carrying on alone. He turned around and screamed at his Lord, just as you or I would do, asking, "Lord, you said that once I follow you, you would never leave me nor forsake me. Where are you, Lord?"

Personally I did not hesitate to scream at my God, "Why me? Why have you left me by myself, Lord?" We all have little faith and would scream at the smallest chance we have to think that we are alone.

This is a prayer and a powerful testimony. I have to talk about these prayers to remind you that everything we need to reach God is always within our reach, but we always take things for granted and blame or question God for our mistakes. Just like the serenity prayer and the prayer of Jabez, we have had this great prayer sitting in our living room for years. It never dawned on me to stop again and look at it. It had become one of the decorative items.

The footprint prayer of testimony was a Christmas gift from a young lady who worked with me several years ago. She said that I had been a big role model in her life and that although she was not an active Christian, she could only find this writing to give me. She added, "Please tell me you like it." Of course I did. At that time, it was a simple gift given with all her heart and was wholeheartedly accepted. After my husband passed away, I would stop to read some of the scripture and words of inspiration that hung all over the walls of our living room. It was then that I stopped at the footprint and read it over and over again. It made sense at one time yet the next time I stopped at it, it was just another inspirational writing. But whenever I felt downcast, I would go back to it. I realized that each time I stood to read it, tears would run down my eyes and I would quietly say, "Lord, lift me up that I may stand, don't leave me by myself, I need you in my life."

Just like the man in the footprint, sometimes life is not fair. Sometimes we wonder if God is really there. Does He know that our burdens have become unbearable? Hey, when my child was sick, did He know that I needed Him? When I am weary and anxious, does God really know? Why would things be difficult for me, why me? When the man in the footprint questioned his Lord just like I did, that was when he was made to realize that during the time of great storm, time of trial and tribulations, time of fear and pain, when he was weary and not able to walk, that was when the Lord lifted him and carried him to safety. His question was his faithful prayers (his heart's desire).

I was told not to ask questions. But I refused. I had the need to know what God was doing with my life. I trusted my life into His hands and when I felt that things were not going well with me, I asked for Him. I advise you, the afflicted, to ask questions. God knows that we do not know why these things happen. He will answer in kindness. Ask as in prayer, with trust and confidence. This man asked and he was uplifted. I must ask in faith and I know that He will uplift me. As we ask, we must realize that we have no right to question God's authority. We are allowed to ask with respect and in prayer when we do not understand. God, being our kind and Heavenly Father, will answer His children.

David was so fed up with problems and he asked God several times what He was doing away from him. When we ask, we let Him know how we feel even though He already knows and understands our pains. David asked in faith for deliverance and it was granted him. In all these three scriptures, we find David asking God **"why me"?**

Psalms 10:1
Why do you stand afar off, O Lord?
Why do you hide in times of trouble

Psalms 13:1-2
How long? O Lord would you forget me forever?
How long would you hide your face from me?
Verse 2
How long shall I take counsel in my soul,
Having sorrow in my heart every day?
How long will my enemy be exalted over me?

Psalms 22:1
My God, my God, why have you forsaken me?
Why are you so far from helping me,
And from the word of my groaning?

David asked questions several times but did not even once question God's authority. Scripture also gives us instances where others, including Christ, asked questions but did not question God's authority. They all asked in faith because they trusted God.

In the book of **Mathew 27:46,**
Jesus asked God at about the ninth hour,
when he cried with a loud voice, saying:
Eli, Eli, lama Sabachthani? Which means:
"My God, my God, why have you forsaken me?"

Our Lord, Jesus Christ asked God why He left him by himself. He was not demanding an answer, nor was he questioning God's authority. His question was an indication that he was tired of suffering in the hands of his enemies. He needed God to bring it to an end. It was enough and he did not want to continue the suffering. He asked God where He was or why wasn't God with him. If you are with me, I would not be suffering, he said.

When we find ourselves in problems such as pain and agony, in any adversity or affliction, we in our human nature have the tendency to forget that we have a promised help. Christians are supposed to realize that God has promised us deliverance if we should turn to Him. If our need for immediate help should warrant asking questions, God will not hold you responsible for that or take any offense in your asking. He only wants us to ask with faith and not by questioning His authority. A faithful prayer is all we need in times of trouble and of such, God will not despise.

I prayed for a long time, seeking my duty to my God. This was not because I could not see what was laid before me, but because I was blinded by my personal needs. I wanted to take care of things my own way. Oftentimes, we feel that our lot from God is so much or so heavy that we wish we could run away from it. There is an old saying that one can never run away from his or her shadow. No matter what responsibility life brings your way, you should know that God would not leave you with more burdens than you could bear. You cannot run away from your responsibilities. It will always be yours. This is where prayer really comes in action. What can we ever do without prayer? As I lined up my list of prayer requests to God, my duty to my Maker was spelled out for me. I began to ask God to make me strong and willing to do the work He has called me for. I asked Him to bless the things that I do and allow me to bless others with it. Whatever I did, I prayed that it will only be to glorify Him.

As I mentioned before, I am grateful to my church family. After several meetings with pastor, Siegried Neuendorff, it was clear to me that things had really changed for me. I had to learn how to juggle two people's jobs in one. It would be my choice to make it for better or for worse. I was determined to do whatever I had to do for better. He showed a fatherly love to my children and me. I found strength in talking with him. After each prayer meeting or Bible study with him every Sunday morning, I reaffirmed my trust in God and my willingness to do my best for my children.

My husband was buried six days before my older son's fourteenth birthday. A few months later, my sixteen-year-old daughter would be seventeen, graduating from high school and going to the university. I also had a twelve-year-old son and a nine-year-old daughter, both of whose birthdays were fast approaching. I knew very well that it was impossible for me to even try to cope with what I had to do. I could not see any sense in anything at this time but surely, there had to be a way out for every problem.

I have heard people say that if you want to play the blues, you must first understand the pain. I am sure that anyone could ask the same question, "How much pain can one have to understand the blues?" Why do we have to suffer in order to understand pain? It seems like for us to understand the ways of God, we must experience some kind of pain or difficulty.

I spent my time looking for every song in the hymnals to comfort me. I found every verse in the Bible for wisdom and knowledge. I learned to have sweet songs in my mouth and prayers in my heart. At one time, my children told me that I made up songs from every statement I made. I guess I sang so much of every song I knew from childhood that they started believing that those songs were not real. They were Mommy's version of some other songs. According to them, my happy songs made them happy too. Occasionally they joined me and made it more fun for the family. I knew that I had to look up to Christ for help, and I prayed and sang it daily.

Turn your eyes upon Jesus
Look full in his wonderful face
And the things of this earth

Will grow strangely dim
In the light of his glory and grace.

The songs that I sang, coupled with the prayer that I said, became my strength. Knowing that God is with me really kept me going, although I was still very skeptical of what life would bring the next day.

I did not know how to run a business, but now I'll have to run our family business. I have never tried to run a family by myself, but now I will have to do that. My daughter is preparing to leave home for the first time. What would college be like for her? How can I be strong for these children? I had to turn my eyes upon Jesus. Although I was determined to do my best, and asked God for guidance, Satan always planted his seed of discord and things would seem better one day and by the next day, it would seem like I had not even started my journey, and it was not going to be easy. I tried very hard in my daily work and was able to carry on without letting anyone know how sore I was in my hurt. Since I hard no reason to beg for food, it was hard for most people to believe that I should have any worries.

Step by step, every ladder was being climbed. Each morning as I prayed, I felt like I could fly like the eagle. I felt like I had everything I needed for the day, but as the day went by, a little doubtful mind took me back to memory. Life was not fair.

Psalm 121
I will lift up my eyes unto the hill,
From whence cometh my help......

My mother taught me how to sing this prayer from the book of Psalms when I was a child. When I asked God where my help would come from, He directed me to look up above and seek Him.

My help comes from the Lord, which made heaven and earth. I must remember that God created everything and He

knows all about me. My help will only come from none
other but Him.

He will not suffer thy (my) foot to be moved.
He that keepeth thee (me) will not slumber…...

These are just but a few of the many promises God has
made me and He was not going to fail me. I knew that I have
a tough job ahead and I was willing to accept it, knowing
that I will never be without God's guidance. I needed support
and I constantly asked God for it in all my prayers.

I know that God's promises never fail and He was not
going to fail me. I had to trust Him. My daughter will go
to the university of her choice. I had already thought about
that and we all prayed about it. As days went by, and weeks
and months went by, pressures of my daily duties continued
to pile up. It seemed like my prayers would not get me
anywhere. We owned a pharmacy, and as a pharmacist,
I had to put in my best effort to keep the family business
running. Between managing the pharmacy and caring for
my children, I thought that I would never live a normal
life again. I was juggling between three schools every
morning to drop of all four children before rushing to work.
Despite prayers and even help from good friends and family
members, life was still not fair at all to me. I could not see
an end to my fears and worries.

To be realistic, it was not easy in any form. As I prayed
more and more, my burden seemed heavier and I could not
understand why.

It is amazing to know that most of my difficult times
came from few of the people who were very close to the
family. I believe that it was not easy for them to accept the
loss of their friend, mentor, or relative, as well as it wasn't
for me nor for my children. One major problem in times
like this is to deal with hypocritical sympathizers. It is hard
to understand society, especially when they mourn for what
they would miss, rather than for the person that they have

lost. Some people may never understand the hurt in the heart of a widow or an orphan. While some people would go out of their way to be exceptionally nice and willing to help and comfort the afflicted, others would totally be out of their senses, demanding every bit of your time and attention for themselves. This may have been so because of the fact that we are traditional people. Certain traditions in certain parts of the world are not obtained in the Western world. Sometimes, a widow lives at the mercy of everyone who survives her late husband. Once a man dies, everything he left behind, including his wife and children, becomes the property of his people surviving him. His wife (widow) does not matter anymore. It really does not matter if she had any children or not. In some cases, everything she has will be taken from her. Depending on the situation of things at the time of her husband's death, she may be allowed to go back to her family with nothing but her children.

Some traditions allow the woman to be married by the next younger or older man (next of kin) in the family. A widow lives at the mercy of those who would support her and her children. This same tradition follows a divorcee. Life, in some traditions, is like a living hell for a divorced woman. She would have to live with the shame of her divorce for the rest of her life or until some other person marries her, and most often as a second wife. She is oftentimes looked down upon and spends her time in loneliness. Those who are afflicted with diseases or misfortunes are cast aside to spend their lives in solitude. Although these things are now changing for the better, it will be hard to completely overlook such tradition, regardless of where the people may be.

In times like this, many things may work together to complicate the situation, but as for me, I refused to give up hope. I did not lose faith in God. Although my faith was weak, I did not lose faith or trust in God. I believed strongly that one day, God would work out a way for me to deal with certain things. I never believed in failure. I knew that come what may, I was going to attain any height that God already planned for my family. My husband and I had always thought about a trust fund in the family name that will help us to help other people. He did not live to see it happen.

My goal was to fulfill this desire of ours. If only I could do this as fulfillment of the desire that burned through our hearts, I would be happy and grateful to my God. I knew that it was not going to be easy, since I had other duties for my family. I was afraid of the stories and news about single parenting, and this was my greatest nightmare. It seemed that every child who misbehaved was a product of a single parent. The televisions, the newspapers, people, and in short the media as a whole, portrayed single parenting as if it was a crime on its own. Of course I was not going to succumb to that. I knew that God and I must do something much better together. Through prayer and supplications, I stayed close to God and He heard my prayers. I refused to bow for the enemy and asked God to hide me and shelter me **(Romans 12:21)** from evil men. I needed strength and courage to deal with these people.

You may never have thought of what life would be like in situations like this. When you feel like you have been tossed up and down by the storm of life. When you have been completely discouraged, thinking that even the tiniest hope has also been snatched away from you. The Bible tells us in times like these to count our many blessings. What are the blessings, and where are they? When tragedy hits and all hopes are gone, the last thing you want to hear is someone telling you that you are blessed. I could not find any form of blessing in my situation. There is no blessing when a loved one is taken away from you. What blessing will a child have in becoming an orphan, or a woman in seeing herself as a widow. Regardless of my disposition, I was able to rely on the prayers of some well-wishers, good friends, and family who relentlessly stayed close and reminded me that God had not finished with me.

Although I have always been a busy person, I found out that I needed more than just going to work to keep me going. I was not going to do anything just because someone else was doing it. I will stay busy because that was the only way I could get by on a daily basis without spending time thinking and warring unnecessarily. I constantly reminded God that I was helpless unless He comes to my rescue. I knew that I could not be a better parent for my children without His guidance. I had to turn my entire life over to my Maker. I asked God to take every moment of my life and guide me step by step. I told Him that I desired my children to be the best, so take them and teach them your ways. I want to be the best mother and single parent that I can be, so take me and teach me to do things right. As I prayed day and night, I felt happy that I had reminded God of my needs. I claimed His promises and waited patiently.

In reading the book of Isaiah, I found a favorite verse.
Isaiah 41:10
Fear not, for I am with you;
Be not dismayed, for I am your God.
I will strengthen you, yes, I will help you,
I will uphold you with my righteous right hand.

I tried to imagine my Heavenly Father telling me to go on and not fear because He is with me. He is strong enough to fight every fight for me. As a little child, there is no greater love or promise than that. When you become an adult and can hear these promises as you read them, knowing that God really never fails in His promises, if you are like me, you will do exactly what I did. I believed and I trusted Him. My God delivered me and made me strong. Yes, I could do all things through Christ who strengthens me.

I started to have more confidence in God's words and promises, knowing that He will never fail me. As though I did not have enough already in my hands, I started to involve myself with what I would call extracurricular activities. They say that children learn what they live. I found it to be true. I was not satisfied with just going to work and running around children in the house. I had to be involved with what was going on in my church, my community, and around me. I went back to school to study naturopathic medicine. Soon my children were no longer satisfied with just coming home from school and finishing their homework. No matter what more I asked them to do, they still had more time for other things. We had rules for certain extracurricular activities such as playing games and watching television. These were set aside for specific times only. The rules were very well obeyed. Like their mother, they all became involved with community work, church activities, and more involved with sports. We became a very active family. Anything that will keep us from having dull moments to set our minds into warring and wondering was the last thing we would think of. We kept up our faith in God and learned to use our time wisely.

I remember that my baby daughter was allowed to sleep with Mommy when her older sister went to the university. Three years later, one night she called me and asked me if I could now sleep by myself. I said yes, but why are you asking? She told me that she could no longer handle the fact that I never go to sleep. She told me that whenever she fell asleep, that I was always awake, and whenever she woke up in the morning, I was awake too. She said that she came to sleep with me to keep me company, so that I would not be afraid of sleeping by myself. Evidently, it was not working, so she was going back to start sleeping in her room. I could not help but laugh. I had asked her if she wanted to sleep with me so that she would not be alone in her room. She did this for three years and I did not know that she was doing it to keep me company or so that I would not be afraid of sleeping alone. Although I actually always kept myself busy, I felt a deep love for this child worrying about Mommy in a time like this.

My typical day was completely full. I would start the morning with a personal prayer for my daily strength. Then I would wake up my children to get ready for school. We did not miss anything that we were used to doing when their father was alive. They knew to pray before meals. After breakfast, we would have our morning devotion. We would pack our lunches and backpacks into the car and would drive off to the furthest school to drop of the oldest child who was in high school, then come back to drop off the two boys in middle school. Our final stop was closer to home, where I drop off the youngest child in grade school. I dropped her off last so she can get longer time to be with me, rather than be in the school long before it opens. After I drop her off, I would then zoom off to work and still try not to be late. This was our daily routine. As soon as I got to work, I would sit down and shed my tears of relief. I call them tears of comfort and relief rather than tears of grief, because the word *grief* always seemed to bear an extra burden on my mind when ever I thought about it. I needed the comfort from the Holy Spirit. Each time I laid my burden at God's feet and shed my tears, I felt like my strength had been renewed. We did not suffer setbacks from illnesses but just the few occasions of minor aches, fever, or pain on any of us seemed like another storm in my life. It was never easy to know that one of us was not feeling well. Missing school or doctor's visits for any of them brought back memories to me. I was constantly on my knees pleading for good health. I did not miss work even one day for reasons of ill health. This was enough to tell me that God was very much in control of my life, but it still took too long for me to know His will for me.

Gradually, I began to realize that I had a duty to perform and that I was not going to be found grumbling or lacking in my duty. I have a family to manage all by myself. God did not consider my little faith but chose me to carry on this duty. How will I do it? What does He expect of me? Is it something that I can really do? I knew in me that I could not, but yet if there is any one thing that I wanted to do so much in my life, it was to do His will. It was to raise my children in the right way and give them the best in their lives that they will never forget nor depart from.

Each new day brought new challenges. I was not going to give up. As I faced these challenges, my faith and hope in God grew stronger and stronger.

Psalms 71:1 In Thee, O Lord, do I put my trust: let me never be put to confusion. On a daily basis, the devil would plant his discord, but I constantly pleaded with God to shelter us from the devil's hands. In every prayer, I asked for deliverance from all dangers and calamities of the world. Friends sometimes seemed like enemies. When you find yourself in this situation, certain behaviors would make you keep a distance from people you had thought had your interest at heart. I prayed to God to weed off all pretenders from my life and my path. The last thing I needed was confusion. I did not need the friendship of double-faced people. If anything would turn me from gaining the promises of God, I asked Him to bind it and cast it away for me.

My prayers gave me strength and as I grew stronger in my faith, I started to accept that God is the answer to all my needs and that He hears my prayers. Things were still pretty tight and I knew that it would be well one day. Finding time to pick the children up from school was another big problem to deal with. They were too young to drive, so I had to do all the driving that was needed on a daily basis. Sometimes my children would, for fear of putting me through stress, not ask for help. By the time I found out, it may have been late but God always sends help from somewhere through someone to intercede. Such help came handy from some of my employees. God used most of them to comfort me.

I would describe some as the kind of people that God sends your way when imminent help is needed. They understood my need for physical, mental and spiritual help. I do appreciate them..

In times like these, we need true love and care, and only those designated by God can afford you such help. Despite some definite obstacles, stumbling blocks, and difficult people, who I called enemies of progress, I had strong relationship with many people in my community. I prayed for such people to come my way and God granted my prayers. I did not allow any day pass by without reading the word of God. The Bible had every comfort or consolation that I needed. I relied on God's promises in my daily living. I found more comfort doing not just my usual daily duty but in doing a little more each day as I met with other people. Talking to someone or doing some things for someone made life much easier. The busier we were, the happier we were. My children loved their sports and this made school more fun for them. They loved participating in community and church works. I believe that in so doing, they too found out the joy of relating to other people in life's walk. It was very rewarding especially since we had the habit of discussing our daily encounters during prayers at night.

Little by little, I found myself listening to other people and their problems. The more I listened to different people, the more I realized what God was doing with my life. I realized that I had the **gift of listening, which comes with patience.** I started to put my problems aside and listen to other people's problems. I oftentimes ended up telling them to trust in God. Sometimes I would sit back to listen to myself, wondering how I did what I did. It was a relief each day to know that I had been able to comfort someone else. I became aware of the fact that God had His eyes on me so that I could keep an eye on someone else. I accepted His promises and claimed His gift for me.

Isaiah 43:2

When thou passeth through the waters, I will be with thee;

And through the rivers, they shall not overflow thee:

When thou walketh through the fire, thou shall not be burned;

Neither shall the flame kindle upon thee

It is a joy to know that God cares for His children. He is there to protect us from all enemies and evil. He is there to guide us through all hard times.

There was always hope for a better tomorrow. Month after month and as the years went by, I realized more and more how much my children needed me in their lives. I tried to hide my feelings to accommodate theirs, only to realize that although they were children, they were doing the same. They watched out for me. They will say or do things just to make me happy or make me laugh. They wanted to know that Mom would be there for them. Just as I would sneak into their rooms to see how they were sleeping, they would do the same to see if I was alive. A few times, they would come to my room and find me sleeping, and they would open my eyes to be sure that I was alive. The youngest child did it so much that it became a joke that I would pretend to be sleeping and refuse to open my eyes. Such things told of what was going on in the minds of people, both adults and children, when tragedy knocks at the door. Even as you hurt, think of the little ones and imagine what they go through. There was never one day that passed that we did not commit ourselves to God. Yes, in times like this we really need a savior to be our anchor. We need to be sure that our anchor will hold and grip the solid rock, Christ our Savior.

Just A Faithful Prayer

CHAPTER FIVE

God Never Fails.

My baby had just turned ten years old and had been going for Bible study. It was time for her to be baptized. This was another difficult moment in our lives. Daddy will not be there to see her get baptized. Several months before, my oldest daughter graduated from high school, and Daddy was not there to see her graduate. Our first son graduated from junior high; he was not there to see him. My second son will soon be graduating from junior high school, and he will not be there to witness it. Every graduation would come and go, and he would not be there. It seemed like every event would bring back memories. This is something we would have to put up with for the rest of our lives. It was obvious now that we must accept things the way they are and carry on with our lives. It would always be easier to talk about these things, but only God knew how painful things were.

It was not just painful to know that a loved one was no longer there to lend a helping hand; the bad part of all these is that even in times of joy, he would not be there either to share in the happiness. There will be many more times of joy and there will be times of remembrances. I could not help but cry, even at these times.

Many people could not understand and would never understand. Some may have stood by the wayside with envy in their heart, wondering how in the world are you surviving. Some may have thought and said a prayer or two for the family. Some claimed their righteousness and superiority while thinking that it was okay, it did not matter; after all, it happens all the time. The truth was that at this time, nothing would make any more difference. The best thing you would do for yourself in times like this would be the decision you make in partnership with God. Although my days were full of tears, I made a decision to submit my life, and the lives of my children and all about us, into the hands of God.

There were times of joy and laughter. Sometimes our joys were cut short by memories. There were times of pain and sickness. Such times were very hard to deal with. I cried through it while doing my best. I never wanted my children to know my weakness. My bathroom and my closet were my best hideouts for crying, complaining to God and praying to Him. I had gone from blaming my God to complaining to Him and finally directing my prayers to Him.

In Psalms 68:5,

God has promised us that:

He is the father to the fatherless, and the judge of the widows.

Thanks to God for His promises.

It was a joyous occasion following my daughter's baptism at the Redondo Beach Seventh Day Adventist Church. Friends and family were there with us to witness the occasion. After her baptism, we decided to move to a church on another side of town. Our current church had become too emotional for us. A few members would still cry and remember my husband each time they saw us. Certain songs and programs that my husband used to lead out on would bring back memories and emotions. We unanimously agreed to move to another church. We searched for churches and found one that we felt comfortable with. Normandie Avenue Seventh Day Adventist Church at this time was very warm and accommodating. We liked being members of this church. My children felt at home and we all quickly made friends with everyone.

I found several members with whom I had one thing or another in common. I made myself open to learning through association with most other women. I found some Christian sisters who were spiritually rich. I became interested in every church activity. The more I associated with more people, the more comfortable I felt and my worries started to be less. I simply maintained a strong relationship with God, praying daily that nothing would separate me from my Maker. Even as I prayed daily and constantly, I was always skeptical of my children's well-being. I asked God to grant me wisdom and courage to train them in the right way.

God never fails, yes, God never fails. As though people knew my need for assurance. I heard this over and over again. Almost every conversation that I had with someone ended with the words, **God never fails.** I was always reminded that God will never allow me be to bear any burden that is beyond my capability. This and many more things never made much sense to me anymore. Many things seemed to bother me. I would frustrate myself with people's attitude. These things were very irrelevant but in times like this, little things magnify. It was just the way the devil wanted to dissuade me from knowing what was right for me.

I was not giving God the chance to handle things for me. Even though I asked for His help, I never allowed Him to step in and carry me through. I needed to learn to let go. I thought that I had it all together. Little did I know that just one thing was missing, and that was for me to lay down my burden of anger. I continued to hear that voice, "God never fails, 'He will never let you bear any burden beyond your capability'; He will never fail you." I believed that, but how long would He wait to deliver me?

I found out that even when, I seemed to be hard-headed and refused to listen to Him, He would still love and care for me. He allows us to deal with our problems the way we deem right. Then He steps in just in time to let us know that we need Him to bear us through. He will not come to you if you do not want Him to. The Bible tells us to ask, and it shall be given us, seek and we shall find, knock and it shall be opened unto us. We must also know that we must ask, seek, and knock in faith before these will be fulfilled. As I pleaded and prayed to God, I still held onto my strong self-will and power. Anger and fear were my major problems. I found out that taking care of my children and dealing with society was not in any form my problems. My children were fine and will remain fine. Society, on the other hand, would not change. My perception of society and responsibilities were my problems. The moment I found out these problems, things took a different turn in my life. I was not going to let the loss of my beloved husband prevent me from meeting him in heaven. I was not going to give in to the devil's deception. My children will not suffer. God has a purpose for us to be here on earth. Whatever God wants me to be, that is what I will be, and what He wants me to do, I will do. I would never stop praying to my God. Even when I think that He had failed me, I would still praise Him.

My pattern of prayer changed. My outlook to the world changed. I started to ask God to give me a new spirit, a spirit of forgiveness and better understanding of what my duty is for Him. I want to let go and I want to have peace in my heart. I was no longer going to be afraid of how to take care of my children. I have given you, my God, all my burdens; take them and let me have your yoke, which you said is lighter. As I prayed differently every day things started to have a different outlook for me. I read every chapter of the books of Psalms, Isaiah, Ecclesiastes, and Job. Although I read other books of the Bible, these four were my main focus. When I needed to learn some advice, I read the book of Proverbs. I remember when I was growing up that we were taught a song that the Bible gives you words of wisdom and the hymns gave the words of comfort. With a faithful prayer in my heart and a beautiful song in my mouth, things started to change the moment I understood and started praying right, hence the beginning of my new hope **(ADVENT OF A NEW HOPE). It is all about a faithful prayer.**

Things did not just happen overnight. We all need to realize that good things do not just come by the way. It took me a long time to come to the level of realization that I could not do or change anything by myself. Sometimes we have to go back to the beginning or to where we started to be able to make adjustments. When there is tragedy or when there is affliction of any kind, we meet with all kinds of sympathizers. Some of these people can be labeled "miserable comforters." Some may come in the form of advisers to tell you what you need to do. Beware, because as one good friend of mine would say, they are better described as "mischievous councilors." Some may come to see where you hurt most so that they would take advantage of you. These are the "enemies of progress." Despite good friends and well-wishers that you may surround yourself with, these negative people will always find their way into wherever there is affliction. I dreaded them and held my anger strongly against these people. I allowed that anger to govern my ways and this was why I could not see what God was doing in my life. If I truly needed Him to rule my life, I had to start praying right. I learned to do so by associating with fellow Christians.

Whenever my stress seemed heavy on me or when I thought that God has not cared enough, I would make sure that I would find room to cry and pray. It was just impossible to hide my tears. One morning, I woke up and realized that I had again been crying in my sleep. I opened my eyes and tears ran down my cheek like water dripping down from a fountain. This was just one of the several occasions that this happened to me. My eyes were all puffed up. I could not hide my face. When my older son asked me, "Mom, did you cry?" I could not lie to him, and not wanting to say no, I said to him, "Do I look like I cried?" He said yes. I told him yes, of course I did. When he asked me why, I felt very ashamed of telling a young child that I was still crying because his daddy had passed away, or because I could not handle my problems. From the look on his face, I thought that I had just reminded him of something that he was trying to put behind him. At this moment, I promised myself that I would never cry again for this issue. Rather than go to bed tossing and crying, I decided to read the many books, cards, and letters sent to me more than a year ago. I did shed a few tears reading them, but at this time, I was able to see deeper and clearer that I could one day praise God and be able to say to someone else, "It is okay, God loves you and He would take care of you." I could tell someone that, "God would never allow you to carry a burden that is beyond your capability." I began to see the goodness in people. It was then that I read my brother's letter again.

We had received wonderful cards and letters of comfort sent by people in condolence when my husband passed away. I kept them all for a few years. One of the letters I received was from one of my younger brothers. This is a brother who, under normal circumstances, would not write. At this time, he wrote. He asked about my children and our health. He said that he had nothing to tell me that could comfort me, but that he had but one story that might help me understand the will of God. He wanted me to understand that God loves me and was still with me.

He wrote that it was up to me to make any meaning out of it or just disregard it. I read this letter and tossed it just like any other card or letter at the time I received it. At this point in time, all these cards and letter came in handy. I was able to read most of them again.

His letter read...in part:

My dear sister,

It could have been worse.

Do not ask why God did this to you. It may or may not be His will.

Recently there was a plane crash in Nigeria. Many souls were lost. A lady had gone overseas to have her last baby. Her husband gathered the rest of the children to welcome her and the newborn as they flew back from England. They boarded the plane from Lagos to fly back to the East. The airplane crashed and everyone perished. They were not the worst of sinners. How would you ask God what happened? I can only tell you to give God glory in everything.

As I read this portion of his letter I thought I had never seen that letter before, but I remembered discussing it with him, yet it did not make sense to me then. This second reading was my eye opener:

Things do not happen to us because we have been spotted out nor because we are the worst of sinners. Although we can ask all the questions we like, the truth is that God never changes. Whatever that comes your way you must take it and still give Him glory because it could have been worse.

Troubles and tribulations come in different forms. No one person has it all good. I have refused to cry, but rather to occupy my mind with meaningful things. As though I was not busy enough with my daily chores, I registered for every seminar that I could find time for. I would go to my professional seminars, meetings, etc. I would go to every religious seminar, church activities, and women's ministries. As I went to these things, I took my children along to some of them whenever possible. Anything that I could do to keep myself busy, I did not hesitate to do it. I did not want to be told sorrow or sorry any more. I began to see things different.

I knew that I could be happy in the things that I do. God spared my life and the lives of my children. We did not all die. There must be a reason why He let us live and there must be a reason why He took my husband home. It was his time to go.

A different kind of fear gripped me. This time it was the fear of what God has in store for me. I wanted to do His will. As I asked God to be with me, I asked Him to take care of those who upset me and keep them away from me and from my children. All I wanted was freedom from the heaviness of heart that followed the loss of my husband. I knew that God is able and He will carry me through this ordeal. I found more strength whenever I read His promises, many of which I found in the book of:

Isaiah 40:31

But they that wait upon the Lord shall renew their strength;

They shall mount up with wings as eagles;

They shall run and not be weary;

And they shall walk and not faint.

I found out that in order to hold up as a single parent, you must be strong or you would be lost in the crowd. I was not going to let my children be one of the numbers. I taught them good behavior, our tradition, and to continue to live in the fear of God. This was the only way we could overcome all obstacles and be able to overcome our enemies. As God would have it, my children were never my biggest problem as I had thought. Up until this moment, they never one day caused me any pains or any reason to regret them. They gave me the reason to work hard and to be happy in what I do.

Two different seminars had taken place in my church. I thank God that I was able to attend these seminars. Each of these seminars—like the letter from my brother—left a lasting impact on me, affecting the way I perceive life. Things that I thought did not mean much were rekindled in my memory to assure me of God's love and expectations of me.

It was a women's ministry day at my church. I had no time at all, but I knew that I must attend this occasion. I promised myself this as a treat. It was a wonderful day, the sermon was great, and everyone was happy. The afternoon section had the biggest impact on me. On a Sabbath day, we had to attend church, but coming back in the afternoon for this seminar was not easy on me. I made sure that I would find time to close the Sabbath that day to my full satisfaction. The seminar was on problems such as mine. It sounded like we were being told to give God glory in everything. O well that is a usual thing, I thought. What else do we need to hear? But the lady told a story of a group of people with all kinds of afflictions. Each one seemed to believe that his or her condition was worse. It sort of reminded me of the grass being greener in your neighbor's back yard. This group of people had complained so much so often that they were called to a meeting that would supposedly alleviate these problems.

They were to be served a cupcake each. But each person would first take a cupcake and write his or her problems on it. They would all put the cupcakes back in the tray. One by one, they were called to go back and pick a cupcake, but not to pick the one they wrote on. Pick a cupcake placed by someone else, read the problems written on it, then eat that cake and the problems on it will automatically become your problems. It was amazing that no one wanted to eat any cakes. As people picked up other people's cupcakes, they swore they would rather have their problems back.

Why? They obviously realized that the grass was no longer greener on their neighbor's side.

As I listened to the story with my hand under my cheek, I tried to visualize my own imagination of "why me or why not." I thought of the family that crashed in the airplane. I thought of several others who may be going through the same problems or who may be thinking just like I am. I came to realize that truly, no one person has it all. As we are different, so are our problems, and everyone has his or her own problems. You must take what life gives you. You must not only take it, but also do something good with it and in good faith. Give God glory, for it could have been worse.

God will never leave you alone. He will always surround you with wonderful people to comfort you. You just have to open up your door to His goodness.

Focusing on the things that delight God was my key to survival, as I was bent on surviving. I gave myself to God and made sure that everything about me must be of Him. I found the need to have good people around me. Through prayer, God revealed to me how I can worship Him and what He has for me. I must stop crying. Tears will not help anymore. I must face reality. It is obvious that a loss of this kind will never be replaced. It surely hurts and cannot be forgotten, but God tells us in His book of love, the Holy Bible, that we should not mourn like people without hope. Where there is life, there is always hope. I was told all these but they never made sense to me until I realized that life is like a wild race and I could not run my race alone. I needed to stop sorrowing or seeking self-pity, and listen to my Father above. The living must have hope or life would be worthless.

It started to make sense now why I must focus on God and stay away from all enemies of progress. Those who comfort should not themselves be miserable. They cannot comfort you if they think that you have something that they envy, miserable comforters. Those who advise and counsel you should not be mischievous or dubious or they will mislead you. Anybody who hates progress cannot wish you well. It is easy to run into these classes of people when you are weak and downcast. This is why I found that prayer and trusting in God is the only way to overcome our adversaries. The world is basically full of these categories of people. Beware of these people. When you surround yourself with godly people and accept God's will, His light will shine in your path to lead you.

I had gone to a seminar in the city of Torrance. I could remember well that the topic was on aging and Alzheimer's disease. I needed this seminar for my continuing education credit. I was not really keen on anything about aging and what comes with it. I was running late because it was not easy for me to find the location. Anyhow, I found the place, but by the time I got there I was about two minutes late. I am one of those kinds of people who would not want to come in when everyone else was seated. This time it seemed like that would be the case. The speaker was just about to start. I quietly came in and stood at the door to locate a seat. I realized then that the entrance was the back door. Sadly enough, there was no empty seat anywhere near. I started to walk quietly toward the front, hoping that there would be an empty seat somewhere. I spotted the only empty seat, in the front. It was the first seat in the second row from the front. I had to walk down through the big hall to the front.

The hall was huge. I did not feel comfortable walking all the way to the front. Every eye would be on me. I had to do it anyway. The speaker had paused, waiting for me to finish my long walk. As I walked toward the front, I noticed that there was a handbag on the chair. As I walked closer, a lady started to remove the handbag from the chair, letting me know that the seat was not taken. I asked her if I might sit there. She cheerfully said, "Oh yes, there is nobody here, it's all yours." I realized that she was much older than I was. About forty-five minutes later, the speaker announced a fifteen-minute break. I had a chance to check out the rest of the people in the hall. It was mostly full of elderly people. It was a seminar for nurses, dentists, pharmacists, and physicians. I believed that more than half of the people there were retired nurses. I was seated on the first chair of the second row in the middle section. I got into conversation with an elderly lady to my left. Through talking to her, I found out why God left that empty seat for me. I wondered why it had to be that seat out of over 200 seats filled with people in that hall. I will call her **Mrs. Jenkins.** Mrs. Jenkins is a name I love of an elderly white lady who babysat my first child. She was a wonderful woman. This new Mrs. Jenkins was another elderly white lady who made an impact in my life. After I met this lady, I strongly solidified my promise that I will live to tell others the things that helped me survive my loss.

Mrs. Jenkins asked me, "How are you?" and I responded that I was fine. I really did not want to talk but I managed to say back to her, "And how are you?" She answered back saying that she was hanging in there. I noticed that she wanted to talk more. I knew that I did not want to talk to anyone at this moment. I looked at her and I said to myself, *You are stuck with this lady, you better talk.* She went on to say that she really did not want to come to the seminar but she could not help coming because she did not want to be home alone. She said that she was a retired nurse and that now she did volunteer work at the hospitals. I knew the next thing would be to ask who I was, what I did for a living, why was I here, and so on. I wished that the fifteen minutes would fly by quickly. Since I could not stop her, I decided to pay her attention and be a friend anyway. Who cares what my problems were, after all I had no reason to lay my burden on anyone. When she realized that I had eased off a little bit and was open for conversation, she let go of everything she had on her chest.

She told me that she was married for forty-nine years and her husband had just died two months ago. She said that she was confused and wished that she had died first. She sadly said that she did not want to live alone. I was able to say to her, "Oh, I am sorry." I went on and asked her if she had children whom she could move in with. She smiled and said that she has a son and a daughter, but she could not move in with them because they were both married with families. Her children lived out of state. She was not willing to leave home after many years of living in the same house with one man. I started to get nervous. I did not want her to ask any more questions about me. The last thing I wanted at this moment was to talk about my husband. I did not want to cry. I knew that the question was coming. I did not want to disappoint her or act silly. She needed someone to talk to and that was the best thing for her. I did not want to talk. I just wanted to keep my burden in my chest. I knew it was too heavy for me but I was blind over what was right for me. It seemed obvious that she would have her way. My fears were confirmed when she said to me, " Are you all right?" I said yes I was. She went on to tell how old both she and her husband were when they got married and how old they were when he died. I had just finished mumbling a prayer for no more questions when she said, "You must be married?"

That was the most uncomfortable question for me at that moment. I answered yes but realized immediately that it was no longer so, and I quickly said, "But my husband died too." She looked at me in dismay, saying, "Oh, no, you don't mean it…. How long ago did he die? He must have been young… You are too young to be a widow." She went on and on. I could not say a word. I was at this time fighting back my tears and at the same time trying to put up a smiling face. I could not recollect what was going on in my head. I just knew that I wanted to disappear right then if possible.

I wanted to change the conversation, so I asked her again what her profession was, and she too avoided my question and asked me if I had any children. I nodded yes, hoping that she would notice my discomfort and stop asking. This lady was not going to stop. She wanted to use the entire fifteen minutes for fact-finding. "Do you have children?" she asked again. As I answered, she handed me a napkin. I said thank you to her. "Yes, I have children and that is my problem. I do not know if I could raise them right by myself." She put her right hand on mine and said, "My young friend, I am sorry." She paused and then continued. The next statement that followed changed the tone of the conversation and the atmosphere around me. She told me that I was strong and blessed. In hearing that, I was about to hush her when she added, "My husband passed away not too long ago. Do you think that I am old enough to take it? No, I am not." She told me that her children were grown and gone and it looked like she would be lonely from then until she died. She went on to say that my situation was even better because I had young children. I said to her, "No, it is better for you when you have no young children to worry about." She continued to tell me that she was now waiting to die, but as for me, I have those four children to keep me going. By the time they are grown and gone away from home, I would have adjusted to my situation. She said that although I will never forget the companionship of a good husband, my children were my blessings and a duty that God had called me to do. She said that the best things I could do for them was to continue to give them my best attention and to love them. The more love I showed to them, the more blessings God would pour on me. It sounded like words I had always heard my mother say to me.

I was just listening now. I was ready to hear more, and of course, she continued. She held my hand a little tighter and said, "You know, there is no better time to lose a loved one. You may have wished that you were married for forty-nine years like me, but after forty-nine years of a happy marriage, you would wish it had happened earlier or not at all." I was speechless, everywhere was calm and the speaker was the only one you could hear after her. It was time to start.

God has a way to unfold His will and desires on us. As I listened to her, it seemed like the entire hall was as gravely silent. Her words of consolation echoed in my ears like the sound of a mighty heart pumping blood after a marathon race. It felt like it would never stop or go away. I must remember those words. I wondered if people were listening; if so, could they have heard her? Do they know how I feel? What would she say next? God knows when, where, and how to comfort us. I can no longer complain because every individual has a cross to carry. Regardless of your age, a loss is a loss and both old and young have their ways of handling such. Finally, I was glad that I met Mrs. Jenkins. Every day of my life, I learned something that I could thank God for.

By now, I have known that I was not left alone. God knew what would happen to me, so He gave me my four children to be my consolation. They are my reason for strength, courage, and wisdom. Just like Mrs. Jenkins had said, they kept me busy, happy, sad, and going. I never had any moment of regret with them. We shared our sadness and joys together. My children are the fruit of the bond that was tied by God when their father and I were united in marriage. If I owed him any respect at all, even though he is no longer here with us this time, I must show it in my children.

Your Heavenly Father will never fail you. It sounds like a joke, but I sang it like a song in my heart every day until I discovered in reality that God never fails. He sends His holy angles to watch over us. He sends His comforter, the Holy Spirit to soothe our sorrows. If He did it for me, He will do it for anyone else who believes. In times like this, what we need is the assurance that life will not get worse. God sends assurance and reveals Himself to you through other people.

I wanted to be the best mother or single mother that I could be, so I made sure that I made myself available for my children and their needs. I made fewer friends, but made sure that I kept a friendly relationship with most people that I met. Most of all, I made sure that my relationship with God was very strong. I gave God my life and those of my children. I gave them a choice to accept God and grow in His light. Those who call me blessed or asked where my strength came from were amazed when they saw the things that I was involved in or able to accomplish. I knew that even in my weakest moments, God made me very strong. He blessed me with good health and gave me the wisdom that I asked of Him. For a period of time, I would occasionally go to my church either very early on a Sabbath morning or stay back at other times after service, just to pray and ask God my heartfelt questions. I was told that a little talk with Jesus made things right. It pleased me to know each day that I talked with God through Christ. It is amazing how each day and in every occasion, God reveals something to His children. We may not see or realize what He is doing for us unless we begin to pay attention to the things around us. A little sermon from a preacher may really turn your life all around for good. God always has good people around us to uplift us in times like this. He will never fail you.

CHAPTER SIX

God's Seed of Equal or Greater Benefit

In 1996, we had a revival seminar in my church. The preacher was a visting pastor from one of our sister churches. As this pastor spoke, he made a statement about good things coming out of adversities. That struck my heart and made me think and wonder. I wrote it down and rehearsed it in my thoughts all day. At the end of that day's revival, I went to him and told him how I enjoyed his sermon. I also found out that there were more people like me listening to him that day. I told almost everybody I knew about that sermon. It was a revival that in fact revived me. He said that in any condition you find yourself, count it all joy. You must give God glory at all times because He is the author of your life and the only one that has control over you.

In Romans 8:28, the Bible tells us that all things work together for good to those who love God, to those who are called according to His purpose.

We all love God, or at least I know I did. Why then didn't all things work well for me? At least it was my belief that something did not work well for me. The word of God said that all things work well together, in which case I now understand that all things both good and bad will work well together for those who love God. I was never going to lose hope in trusting God. Hearing this sermon and many other uplifting sermons made me realize that there is no better place to be found in times like this than in the hands of God or with those who know God. Although I had read most of these Bible verses before and known about them, it made a whole lot of difference to hear them again in sermons, especially at the time that I was going through my storm of life. A little walk with Christ, a little talk with Christ, a little prayer every day will carry you on and place you above all your problems. Just knowing that you have Christ in you will give you the joy you need.

Most Christians these days tend to have been spoiled by the abundant love that has been bestowed on us. We have taken so much for granted that we simply want to wake up each day and say we claim God's promises. Does saying "I know you are there for me" mean you have to be there for me? No, it does not mean so. We claim God's promises by our trust, obedience, faith, and love to Him. When we express all these for God, His blessings will then flow upon us. By taking things for granted I mean that we just simply assume that everything is there for us, so why do we have to suffer or why do we have to ask for it again? Just like we have revivals for our churches, we all need personal or spiritual revivals too. Revival of our souls to help us recognize when and how God talks to us. We are supposed to look beyond our problems and recognize God's willingness to comfort and uplift us from it. According to the **Second Epistle of Peter, 3:9**, God does not want the death of a sinful man. In fact He does not want us to suffer at all, so it is not appropriate for us to blame Him when things go wrong. Rather, we should trust Him and believe that He will make it right for us.

The seed of equal or greater benefit is the fulfillment of God's promises that He will never leave us or forsake us. He will make sure that we are comforted. He will uplift us and will even go as far as satisfying us beyond our expectations. Remember the saying that **WHEN THE MASTER IS GLORIFIED, THE SERVANT IS SATISFIED**.

Isn't it wonderful that we have all these promises from the very one that made us. He is willing and ready to satisfy us with even more than we asked. We must glorify Him by trusting, obeying, and having faith in Him. Only the Holy Spirit can help us turn our misfortune to fortune. By attending several revival seminars and prayer meetings, Christian women's ministry functions and many other Christian religious functions, I was spiritually revived.

Revival seminars brought back memories to my heart. As a young woman, I dreamed of what life would be for me when I grew up. Like most other young people, I wanted the best life could give. I knew the kind of man I would want to marry. I wanted to have many children and to have a happy home. I wanted the best in education. I envisioned taking a happy walk with my husband when we got old. I wanted to be the best mother and wife, and if not in all things, that God's love will be manifested in everything about me. Yes, things were looking great. I thought that my dreams were about to come true when suddenly things turned around 360 degrees. A happy home, a hard-working mother, a loving wife, all just seemed like history in my life. At least that was my thought at the strike of tragedy. I became a widow. I became a single parent. I became the head of the house. I had to make decisions for the family and of course I would have to raise my four children without my husband. I thought that this was the end of the world for me. The man I would walk the street of gold with had gone. I sat in this seminar, and was eagerly listening and hoping that something would happen to make me feel better.

Buried in my thoughts, I was flipping my Bible, searching for some scriptures when I heard him say the very statement, the magic word that turned my hopes around and gave me the strength that I have today trusting what God can do. As I heard him say, **"In every adversity God plants a seed of equal or greater benefit."** I was startled, my heart jumped and I thought I did not hear him right. If I did, I needed some sort of explanation. I thought he knew about my plight. This might be my best text. If it is true, then I hope on it and know that God will surely plant that seed for me. The seed of hope maybe and I will no longer have to worry. I wondered what the seed may be like. What kind of good will come out of adversity? Why was there adversity in the first place? I am not sure, but if it is true, then I will claim it. I started thinking of God as a farmer. I remembered one of my childhood songs that says:

We plant corn and vegetables and beans.
All because God himself is a farmer.
All these grow at night when we are sleeping
All because God himself is a farmer.
Give him great thanks give him great honor
Shout, and shout for joy.
And say all glory be to God, the farmer.

He is a seed planter. Every seed He plants grows. They blossom and they bring forth beautiful fruits. God's fruit is the fruits of the spirit. His plants bring forth enviable fruits, and whosoever shall eat of these fruits of the spirit shall also live and prosper.

The Bible tells us in the book of Genesis that God plants seeds. He is a farmer and we can see this from His beautiful Garden of Eden. After planting, there is always time for harvesting. In the book of **Genesis 2:8,** God plants the Garden of Eden, and in the book of **Revelation,** He tells us about the end time harvesting. Yes, as I listened to the rest of the seminar that day, all my heart could tell me was that there will be a mighty seed planted for me and that the harvesting will be great. I must accept it and I know that God will do it for me. I immediately believed in God's planting of seeds of equal or greater benefit. Only those who believe and accept would have it.

As I searched through the word of God, I found His abundant love and the love of Christ. Sometimes it is hard for us to see what God is doing in our lives. The devil blindfolds us and makes us see only what we think that God has not done. It was hard for me to see what God was doing in my life because I was dwelling mainly on the fact that I had become the widow that I did not want to be. Despite all odds, I continued to ask God to show me at least one thing that will carry me on day by day that I may not go astray. He showed me several ways, one of which was to learn to trust Him. He made me know that a seed of equal or greater benefit had already been planted for me and I had no reason to continue asking questions like I had no hope. I had no reason not to be strong in my faith. I had no reason not to claim my seed and rejoice in the harvest. God's seed will grow regardless. He who waters our plants even when we don't know will of course water His very own seed that He planted. I surely longed for the day I will rip from God's seed. I knew then that with time, my wound would be healed. The scar may still be there to remind me what I had gone through, but there will be no more pain. There would be joy in the morning.

God does not discriminate. He plants this same seed for everyone in every kind of adversity. Only those who believe and accept will claim the victory over adversity. No matter what you are going through in life, God is always there for you. We need to stop laying blame on something or someone and just trust in God. The only assurance we have is in God. Focusing on God through Christ His only begotten son is the only way we can get out of our trouble in this world. He is the only one who can cleanse us and forgive us our sins. He is our comforter and redeemer. Sometimes when we pray, we need to think deeply into what we are saying to God. We should not forget that He knows every need of ours. We tend to ask like we are telling Him what He does not know. We cannot lie to God about our needs. Until this day, I have always prayed for God's seed of equal or greater benefit. No matter what you are going through, remember that **in every**

adversity, God plants a seed of equal or greater benefit. I know that God will plant that seed for you, and you too will harvest your seed someday.

I very much wanted to know what was expected of me. Talking to other people was of great help, but I resolved to searching through the Bible. I wanted to know more about the widows of the Bible.

Sometimes, we need to experience certain things in life to be able to really know how they feel so that when we open our mouths to criticize, we would most likely be mindful of what we are doing. This does not mean that we have to experience every odd to comprehend the pain that comes with it. I looked at the people with similar experiences and imagined me in their position, trying to do exactly what they did, which was to have faith and trust in God. This gave me the hope that all will be well.

The Widow of Zarephath
In the book of 1 Kings, 17:8-24, God commanded Elijah and he went and saw this widow at the city gate gathering sticks. Elijah asked her for some water to drink. She was about to bring him some water to drink when Elijah called again for a little morsel of bread. She was willing to give the last bit of food in her house to a stranger. Although she realized that this was the last food left for her and her son to eat, she calmly responded to Elijah's request, saying, "Surely, as the Lord thy God liveth." If it was God's will, she would do it. Are we willing to do God's will? She was gathering sticks to make the last food left for her and her son to eat and live. She may have prayed all the time for God to help her and her son. When the stranger requested of her food, she was courageous enough to say, "As the Lord liveth." Elijah did not just ask for water and food. He was bold enough to demand that his food should be served first. Seeing her faith, Elijah then told her that according to

God's word, she would never lack food throughout the days of drought. God's words never fail. She believed Elijah's words and trusted in God. She gave all that she had, that a stranger may eat. She did not hesitate in doing what the man of God said. Because of her faith and trust, God provided for her in time of need. I prayed to God to give me the courage to trust Him, as this widow did even in her adversity.

Many Christians these days would take Elijah's words for a joke. We would look at Elijah as being arrogant and inconsiderate. He had the audacity to demand the last bit of food from this poor widow. Sometimes challenges of life come to us in forms we could not imagine. This widow had already given up in life. She was ready to die. She could have refused Elijah's request, since life did not matter to her anymore. In her trials and tribulations, she had probably asked God to intervene by letting her and her son die. God heard her cries and sent Elijah her way. He knew that she was a woman of great faith. He sent Elijah to her so she and her son would not die. She listened to the voice of the man of God. She trusted God and was faithfully ready to obey Elijah as long as he was of God. She was saved. She was able to combat poverty. She and her son had enough to eat for the rest of their lives.

Do we, Christians of this present day, have such faith? Are we able to take pains even the pain of hunger no matter how heavy it is just for us to serve some other hungry person? This story of the widow of Zarephath fascinates me. It is a story I knew from childhood, but as I read it over and over again after I became a widow, I began to understand her plight much more than I did before. It taught me that if I could have but a little faith in God and stand firm in my belief of what He could do for me, I would have no room to contend His blessings. God moves in a mysterious way to perform His miracles. If only we could have the faith of the people of the Bible, we too could move mountains. I know that God had something for me, and I asked for it with wisdom. I was persistent in my prayers and willing to bless others with any blessings God would give me. **Sharing and contentment became an important part of my life.** Never to say no when I could have said yes in times of need.

The Widow with the Two Coins

When we see the impact of faith in our relationship with God, we would realize that no matter what may come our way, He would surely see us through.

As I said before, the Bible became my reference book. I turned to it every time I needed comfort or advice. Although I listened to friends, family, and well-meaning people, I still turned to my Bible any time I had the opportunity. The story of the widow with two coins brought me to my knees. It sounded unreal. I was at a point of saying, "no I can't" to certain things when I realized that my circumstances were not enough to exonerate me from my obligations to my God or fellow man.

In Luke, 21:1-2 and Mark 12:41-44, this widow gave two coins (a widows mites) as her offering to God. Why did she do this, knowing that those were her last two coins? She knew that she had nothing else left in the house. She did not consider this but thought first of what she could offer to her Maker. Somewhere in the back of her mind, she probably thought about God's blessings on her and said, "I know that my God is able and will carry me through." She had complete trust in God and that in no time, He will bless her with more. Or maybe she thought that she would die of hunger and what was the point not giving back to God what was left of her? Her coins were worth less than pennies.

We do not know why we go through certain problems in our lives. Some adversities or afflictions may be just a trial of our faith. When we have not and could not, how much trust could we place in God and know that He will surely provide for us? It may not make sense to someone who really knew me to accept the fact that I cried and prayed for God's grace on me and my children. Some may have seen me as one that had it all. But to such people I would gladly say, "if it were not for the Lord on my side, I do not know where I would have been". When a child comes home from school with holes in his shoes and refuses to ask for a new pair because he or she is afraid that Mother, a widow, might not be able to afford a new pair. When a child refuses to say that he or she is hurting for fear of taking Mom's time out of a busy schedule. When the family settles for a less expensive commodity because they could not afford more. When you the afflicted decide to forgo many comforts for the sake of your children. Friends may decide to look down on you, or people may ridicule you because you have not. These and many more are some of the unspoken heart pains that most men and women, widows or widowers, divorcees or people stricken with poverty, go through in life. Although I would always say that I never had a reason to say that we did not have, I must say that several times, I sacrificed my comfort for the comfort of my children. This was done with no ill feelings, because I understood my obligations with them. How many of us today are willing to sacrifice for others while waiting on God to bless us. I knew that I had to try harder than this widow because she had nothing and was able to give faithfully.

This widow said to herself, *I will give all that I have to God because I know that He is able to carry me through.* Are you willing to give up a little piece of your wealth to God or to those who do not have? I had to submit my life to God several times thinking about these women and knowing that if I could have as little faith as they did, I would be praising God all my life.

Many Christians—and I say Christians because we are dealing with faith at this time—would act differently. We all would want to save for tomorrow. Although we say that we trust God, this situation would pose a problem for most of us. This woman did not only give cheerfully but gave with all her heart regardless of her adversity. I learned from her that no situation is able to deprive anyone of the love of giving. **It is through giving that we receive.** Start from those around you. Give to your family, extend to friends, and gradually carry it on to even people you do not know. While you give, remember to give to the Lord, your God. The widow became my role model. At any time in life, God expects us to do our portion, our duty with Him and with our fellow men while we hope for His abundant blessings on us.

If these widows would trust God so much and give the last of what they own, why should I not have faith in God, knowing that He will even do more for me? He never left them alone and He did not forsake them. God's seed is always of greater benefit. These widows praised God even in their weakest moments. They surrendered their lives to God and He blessed them and wiped away their tears. As for me, I will praise my God, my Maker, while I have breathe. Even if the world should turn against me, I'll still praise my Maker, who of course is greater than the world.

PART TWO

CHAPTER SEVEN

It Could Have Been Worse

A perfect submission to Christ brings a perfect delight regardless of life's circumstances. We must work together with our Heavenly Father for our own interest because it is only by His grace that we can be delivered from evil. When it seems as if nothing is working right or that all is against you, remember that it is then that you need God the most.

The second part of this book deals mostly with my encounter with the world outside of my own little domain. I found out that interacting with other people was one way of relieving myself of the pressures of adversity. People suffer from one thing or another. Some people are afflicted by sickness, others by great losses, or by poverty and hate. Regardless of what kind of adversity, the only hope we have is in God through Christ our Savior. Anything could have been worse, but with God, all things work together for good. I needed to get out and exercise my faith. I started visiting with many widows, widowers, single parents, orphans, the sick and bereaved families. These visits were more rewarding and gave me the opportunity to witness to others. I saw that people would always need each other. It was not always pleasant but it brought me closer to the people who needed to be comforted. I did not want others to dwell on "Why me?" I wanted people to know that no matter what may come their way, God will always be there for them. It was my way of sharing God's love. I wanted the people who are hurting to know that I had been there. It was a way of relieving my heart of the burden of anger and fear. As I visited more people and told of God's love on me and my family, I gained more strength and courage to deal with most things in life. I would invite people to spend time (hours) just to talk with them about their experiences and of course to share with them how I have overcome. It was amazing to know how much people store at heart and brood over in their lives. People did not only need each other, they also need the Lord. It was through these experiences that I found myself as an inspiration to others.

I started to open up more to people. As I came closer to people's lives, I realized how much the relationship has benefited me. I began to see myself not as someone who needed comfort, but as one who could provide it. Whereas once before, I could not even mention the word "death" without breaking down in tears, I now have the courage to mentor others through my faith and trust in God. I no longer saw myself as singled out to suffer but rather to lead.

I know that nothing again would stop me from my present habit of faithful prayer and complete trust in God. I knew my goals: To be the best mother I could be to my children. I wanted to help all widows and orphans who needed help whenever I could through prayer. I wanted to be able to help other people to overcome difficult times by witnessing to them of God's goodness. Finally, I would be able to help people to recognize who they are and uphold their self-esteem believing in God.

People are hurting from day to day. All over the world and around, people are praying and hoping. We need to reach out and touch someone. It is not just to be spoken but we should be practical with things of life. I interacted with men and women of all races, and have come to the conclusion that perception levels are completely different in every adversity. The hurt may be the same, but levels of perception and acceptance may be different due to ethnicity, race, or tradition. Women, of course, suffer adversities very differently from men. I interacted mostly with women and I found out that besides ethnicity, race and tradition, age makes much difference in levels of perception in difficult times. Family background and the involvement of children may also contribute much to ways and levels of perception. In some cases, absence of children may make things even worse. We should not take things for granted. God knows what He is doing. You will find that no matter what may come your way, He already has waged that flow of disaster from complete destruction. I will show abstracts of experiences of different people as I compared it with my personal experience. Whatever your experience may be, I pray that these abstracts would help you to know that only the joy of the Lord can be your strength. Do not be weary. If you believe, you can do all things through Christ who strengthens you.

Sometimes the devil will want to get us by reminding us of our problems. The devil may go as far as letting us know that we are completely alone and that it is going to be rough. The devil wants to see us cry and hands down on everything. In times like these, I learned to turn to the numerous verses in the Bible that gave me strength.

You are not alone

These are true abstracts or testimonies gathered from my encounters with people. The names in these abstracts have been changed for identification purposes. We should never claim to be alone. God wants us to know that He is always with us and that His angels are always watching us. In your tribulations, I want you to know now that you are not alone. I learned and became strong by close contact with other people who were afflicted, and I want you to know that realizing that we need one another in this life's ordeal is the first step to overcoming. When you start appreciating others, your faith in God will grow stronger.

These stories will reveal to us the deeper and innermost feeling and challenges of most people. Afflictions may include death in the family (a loved one), sickness in the family (terminal disease), divorce or separation, loss of a job especially for the head of the family, which may induce poverty, hate, anger, depression, or mere inferiority complex. It could range from the simplest thing we could think of to the most painful. What some people might see as simple may be dreaded by others. Some may agonize over many children in the family while some are praying and begging for even one. I started to document some of these interactions when it dawned on me that there are people out there who need to know how wonderful God is. There are even Christians who need to know what God can do for them. I realized that most of us say we are Christians, yet we do not know what it means that Christ died for us. We ask questions even when it is not necessary. We mourn like we have no hope…hope for heaven. We bear grudges like we have our own lives in our hands. We hold on to our own thoughts like we own the world. We would not let go. We are angry, afraid, hateful, miserable, and withdrawn from society as if the world owes us something. All we need is Christ in us. "People need the Lord" is a popular saying. Once we find Christ, all the anger, fear, hate, misery, and depression will **gradually** be gone. I thought I had it bad until I spoke up and found what God had in store for me. I found abundant blessings in knowing God. If He is kind enough to allow His only begotten son, Jesus Christ, to die on the cross for any of us sinners, what more can't He do to make life worth living for us? "In every adversity, He plants a seed of equal or greater benefit."

Mrs. Jenkins

Let us go back to the story of Mrs. Jenkins as we previously read in chapter six. That was the first testimony that sort of brought me to know that there was no point complaining or wishing against hope that things should not have happened, or that it could have been at a different time.

Mrs. Jenkins was an elderly woman whose children had all grown and left home. Her son and daughter had grown, married, and left home. She had four grandchildren. At this age, when they needed each other most, her husband died. Here I was, sitting next to her wondering why at my age, my husband who was much younger, would die and leave me with four young children. How could I handle this? How could Mrs. Jenkins afford to live alone? Such is the mirth of life.

In talking with Mrs. Jenkins, I realized that I could not change anything by myself. God knows why He allows certain things to happen when they do. I could not tell what life would be for me if I were to be in Mrs. Jenkins shoes. I thought that she had no problems living alone and not having children to raise by herself. By the same token, she thought that I was lucky to have children to keep me company and that by the time they become adults, I would have gotten used to my situation. Either way, we were both right. I know that I received some encouragement from talking with her. Her comments helped me to see my children as my source of comfort and company. Although my mother had always consoled me with the same comments, I had always thought that it was just a mother's way of comforting her daughter. How could it be joy when joy has been cut abruptly? But you know what? God is wonderful. He gave me my children for my joy. And to this day, they have been my joy and my love, care, and of course my worries about them is still strong. I no longer worry in fear but in love.

When I left the seminar, I thought that meeting Mrs. Jenkins was the best thing that happened to me that day. That was the last time I saw her.

Ted's wife
She was a twenty-six years old, the young mother of two children, ages two years and nine months. Little Angela

would always ask for Daddy, says Ted's wife, Monica. Little Ted Junior knew nothing about Daddy's passing. I did not know Monica before this time. Someone had just called me to please go and speak with her. At this point in my life, people had started calling me from time to time to go and talk to recent widows, widowers, divorced and battered women. It got to a stage when I would be called to talk to children or even husbands and wives.

I went to Monica and found out that I was still weak in my own distress. She cried bitterly. I found myself sobbing with her. Ted died in a car accident. His wife says he was a wonderful husband. She could not imagine herself as a widow. They were married for four years. She could not stop crying. In asking, she told me her major problems:

—I hate everyone I see; of course, they do not like me anyway.

—I do not want to see most of his friends, they remind me of him and he is not here.

—Why are people trying to be nice to me? I cannot understand it.

—What will I do with these children? Please tell me, how did you handle your own situation?

—I cannot sleep at night and I am no use for these kids.

She was ready to go on and on but I stopped her. She held her head with both palms and when I asked why, she complained of a pounding headache. Monica was much younger than I was when my husband died. I thought about Mrs. Jenkins and myself, but no, it is different.

"Slow down, Monica I said, God will help you. Everything you complained of, I also went through. You are not alone. I will tell you how I survived my situation."

Her concerns brought back memories to me. I hated to see those who looked at me like some terrible thing had happened to me. I felt like I was not supposed to show my face in public anymore. I remember not being able to comprehend why people wanted to be nice to me. I remember asking God what He wants me to do with my children. I remember those sleepless nights when I would lie still on my bed wondering why life was not fair. I remember waking up in the morning and nothing but tears would run from my eyes down my cheek. As I listened to her, I thought of her age and her very young children. The baby does not know his father. The two-year-old wants to see Daddy. Just the nagging questions, "Where is my Daddy? When is he coming back?" are enough to make you crazy.

My nine-year-old wanted to know when Daddy would come back from his trip. When he did come back, he did not make it through the next day. I could only answer that I did not know to her questions. I know that it was not going to be enough answer for her. Telling her that he went to heaven incurred more questions about death or dying, heaven, and even why God wanted him. I explained to Monica that her fears were not unfounded. I told her to trust in God. Through prayer, your fears will be conquered. We held hands and prayed together.

The promise that I would always be in touch with her was the best part of our meeting that day.

I gave her some Bible verses to read and pray with, one of which is my favorite:

Psalms 121:
I will lift up my eye unto the hill, from whence cometh my help,
My help cometh from the Lord, which made heaven and earth…

As I was leaving her, I noticed a look of doubt on her face. I turned around and said to her,

"Everything will be all right." She said to me, "How long shall I pray and wait? Till the kids grow up?" I answered yes, and even beyond. She nodded her head with disbelief.

I have always been in touch with Monica. She needed someone other than just a family member to talk with. She needed someone who had been through the same path and understood the agony of such loss, and she found that person in me. Because she is very young, I have kept a close relationship with her as a source of encouragement. She is a believer in Christ and she is doing very well.

The Duke Family:

People react differently to different or same situations. Although our problems may seem alike, our reactions to these problems are mostly geared towards our personal needs. People's perception of problems are more so because of what their priority may be. Mrs. Duke has three children, ages four, six, and eight. Her husband, Andy, died at the age of thirty-eight. Mrs. Duke was thirty-five years old. When I spoke to her the first time, she was very bitter and said that life had no meaning for her anymore. She expressed all the anger, frustration, and sadness that go with the loss of a husband. I said, "Well, that is normal." I would be worried if she had expressed otherwise.

Two years earlier, she had lost a baby. She was not happy at all. She could not find any joy in anything she did. She was always angry with herself and her children.

The second time I visited their home, she told me that she did not think that God would answer her prayers. She said that she needed someone to lean on. I said immediately to her, "Lean on Christ." She was quiet for a moment and then said, "I cannot do this by myself, I need help, I need a husband." I asked her if she thought that it would be to her advantage to subject her children to this new father or stepfather at this time. She replied that it did not matter.

She only wanted to be happy. She believed that her children could handle her new husband better than she could handle not having one. Each time we met, we prayed. At this time, we prayed that if it is the will of God, let Him show her the right man who would love her and her three children. She only went to church occasionally. I encouraged her to read the Bible. The more I visited her or spoke to her on the phone, the more I realized what a sweet person she could be.

Mrs. Duke complained:

—Of fear, of loneliness, and of failure in raising her children.

—That she could not trust God. First she lost her child and two years later she lost her husband.

—That she was not financially capable of supporting her family.

— Of anger, frustration, hate, and depression.

She was withdrawing from people. She thought everyone else was better than her. I knew that I had to do something to make her feel better. I started to tell her how I felt a few years ago when my husband died. My situation was not far from hers, although I never wanted to marry again. My children were my priority. Everything I did or prayed for was that God would make me a better person for my children.

I told her how I juggled between housework, schools for my children, and my business. She had to understand that she was never alone. There are many people in the same situation and God cares for all these people, including her.

The greatest comfort anyone would need would be from the Holy Spirit. You must learn to trust God and have faith in Him. Several times, I would see Mrs. Duke and she would look at me and smile, saying, " Hello, strong lady, do you know you are making me strong like you?" I would tell her to keep on praying. One day, she called me and said, "Thank you for being who you are to me. My children are doing well and I know that you are right, God is good."

In times like this, we need each other. No one person can do it alone. I ask God to allow me to be His witness to others as to how wonderful He is to those who believe and trust in Him. As I witnessed for God, I found out how much I had been blessed and never knew it. Now she goes to church regularly and finds joy in talking to other people about herself. She is happily married to a young fellow from her church. "He loves me and even calls my children his children too," says Mrs. Jacobs, as she is known now. Her prayers were answered.

Angie's divorce:

It was cold and windy that Sunday evening in mid-April 1994 when Angie came to visit me. I had wished that no one would visit at that hour. I was not willing to entertain any visitor. But the look on this lady's face pierced through my heart like a sharp thorn. My husband had just died about six weeks ago. The surge of people in our house had started to subside. My children were beginning to adjust to a normal life, I thought. As for me, it would take a lifetime for me to even adjust, if ever I would. The silence that trailed us each time we came home had died down. We had just started to talk louder and normally again. As she walked into the house, the phone rang. I picked it up. I had forgotten that my children did not want me to pick up the phone again for the same reason that something might be said to make me cry. Within seconds, I was crying. The caller had just heard of late that my husband had passed away and was calling to give condolences. My little daughter walked slowly to my side and slid a napkin into my hand. A few minutes later, everywhere was calm. My children went into their rooms to allow Angie and me a chance to talk.

Angie came and sat by my side and said in a low voice, calling me by my middle name (showing intimacy), "Do you know you are a blessed woman?" I thought that she was out of her mind as I looked at her in awe. How could she come at this time in my life to tell me that I am blessed? She nodded her head and said, "Yes and I mean what I said." I asked her why she thought that I am blessed. She said to me, "You were married to your husband for twenty-two years, right?" I said yes. She nodded her head. She looked very depressed. Then she said, "And he was good to you, he saw you as a good wife and your family was a happy one, right?" I answered yes. Tears started rolling down her eyes. Soon we both were crying. Angie said to me, "Stop crying, I should be the one crying, and I need you to say sorry to me." I knew that she was divorced but could not understand what her problem was at this time. When I asked, she in a nutshell told me her life story in a twinkle of an eye. Her marriage was a living hell. She sobbed heavily. Her children were not doing well. She blamed it all on the bitter divorce she went through. I was deeply touched when she said that if she had married someone like my husband for only two days and he died, she would have been better off in life than to go through what she suffered in the hands of her husband for twenty-five years. Such a statement would demand pity from anyone who heard it. I looked at her, shook my head, and said to her, " I am very sorry." Although I said to her that I was sorry for all that she had gone through, I still did not understand why she would cherish a short but happy marriage like mine. If it were so good, why would God allow it to end so abruptly? Three years later, after I had met and talked with several single parents, I began to understand what many women go through in their marriages.

Angie was a victim of a very unhappy marriage. After her divorce, she felt that life had nothing for her. She wished that she could start all over again and make things better. Of course, everyone wishes to start all over again when things go wrong. Angie was not wishing to start her marriage over again. She was wishing to start a new life of no marriage of any kind. Her stories were very sad. According to her, it was a marriage that was never meant to be. She gave it all her time and all she could, yet it failed.

—She lacked confidence in herself.

—She could not trust anyone, even her family members.

—She had a very low esteem of herself

—She was very bitter. Anger and frustration overtook her.

—She was looked down upon by this ex-husband, so she was afraid of getting into any form of relationship with people.

—She could not understand her children's reaction to her problems.

—Angie was always seen as a quiet but bitter person. She would rather withdraw from people because she was afraid of offending them.

I was more worried when she told me that seeing the traits of her ex-husband in her children made her life more miserable than ever. I told her that I was sorry for all that she had been through. She would live with this trait for the rest of her life. Something had to be done and done quickly. She needed the intervention of the Holy Spirit to uplift her. We prayed together before she left. I could not stop wondering why she made that visit. I thought that I should be the one receiving comfort, but she strongly said to me that I should be happy. She wanted me to say sorry to her. I know that there is more to her pains and statement than I could imagine at that time. Angie wanted to talk to someone. She was battling with a major problem but she found time to come to comfort me. The weight of the problem she bore made her see me as even better than her in my own adversity. We all need one another in life's struggles.

A few years after Angie's visit to me, although I had met her in places after that, she approached me again and reminded me that I was blessed. This was a chance for me to tell her something. She asked about my family. I told her we were fine. I asked her about her family; she smiled at me as if to say, *What do you expect?* As though I was waiting for another of her questions, she asked, "How do you do it? Tell me." I quickly thanked God. It was an opportunity for me to witness for God.

I told her how I too have been hanging in there like everyone else. I did not wait to let her know that life is rough for a widow. I told her all my problems. I let her know that I am a single parent too, and the only help my children have. I only survive by trusting in God through Christ, who is my rock and my salvation.

I told her that I pray every day for God to show me that right way to go. I pray for help and I meet good people every day. I do not tell everyone my problems. I went on and on and when I finally said that I would do my best for my children she stopped me and said, "That is one of my problems. How can I get my children to understand what I am going through?" There was no strong relationship between her and her children.

One of the major problems we have in life is of blaming someone else when things go wrong. We always would say, "If God loves me, why would He let me suffer?" We think that everyone else had it better than us. I did not hesitate to let Angie know that I too have had it rough and that I live by the grace of God. She had anger and animosity over her ex-husband. The bitter divorce she went through was always fresh in her heart. She would not let go. She sees her enemy, her ex-husband in her children. This made those children very vulnerable to all her negative emotions. As she saw the children as part of her problems, they saw her not willing to be who she should be, a mother to them.

Angie needed to let go of some anger. She needed to trust someone. She needed the Lord, Jesus Christ in her. She needed a friend who understood, who would let her know that God has abundant blessings for those who trust in Him. I told her that whenever one avenue closed in life, God opens another one for us to go through. I told her about the sermon, "In every adversity, God plants a seed of equal or greater benefit." We spoke at length. Finally she said to me, "Thank you so much for your time, I've always thought you had it easy or that I am the only one having a hard time."

Although our problems were different, we can see that no matter what we do or encounter in life, we all need each other. As we need one another, we also need Christ in us. Many people are wasting for lack of knowledge. It might be as simple as the knowledge to know that they are loved or that they are not alone. I will not fail to give that knowledge whenever I have the opportunity. I had to let go my anger, fear, frustration and misery through faithful prayer. I tell everyone I know that prayer is the first step towards breaking through adversities. It is hard to pray for and love your enemies, especially if they had been an intimate part of your life. You cannot understand why they have suddenly become unfriendly. When a wonderfully beloved spouse turns into a bitter archenemy, life becomes hard to comprehend. Sometimes people carry the agony at heart and suffer for a long time. In our society today, some traditions still look at divorce as a terrible thing, especially on the side of the female spouse. The woman suffers the shame and oftentimes ends up being the one to care for the children. With all these in mind, Angie felt like life was not worth living.

When she realized that she was on the wrong track and started to see her children as her precious gifts from heaven, she put everything behind her and the joy of the Lord became her strength. Angie has a quiet and reserved personality. She always had a dainty outlook to life. When I saw her last, she said to me, "You know what, God is good and I thank him for bringing you my way." Her children are all grown now and have moved away. At age fifty-eight, she devotes her time volunteering at local hospitals while she maintains her part-time teaching job.

Mark: Life is not fair.

In June of 1999, Mark and Betty had only been married six years. They had one child, a son, and his name was John Mark. Betty had just been diagnosed with breast cancer. The news of her cancer was devastating to the family. One month later, it was obvious that Betty would not survive the sickness. They were a young couple and John was only five years old. I was very sad when Mark told me about it. When you meet Christians like these and in times of trouble, you most likely would promise to pray for them. From all points of view, Betty would not make it. I offered to pray for them. For some reason, either from my own point of view or intuition, I constantly prayed for Mark and his little son to be comforted. As for Betty, she had already accepted her fate as it was and given her life over to God. Accepting death was not a problem for her. When nothing could be remedied, the best thing is to accept it and ask for God's intervention and deliverance. The last words I heard from her before she died were, "Heaven is my home, I know that I am in good hands." She was a Christian and believed that Christ was her personal savior.

Betty's death was heavy on Mark's heart. At first he could not handle it. Friends and family were there for Mark and his son. Betty was ill for a short time only, and it seemed like a bad dream that she could so suddenly pass away. Her death was a threat to Mark's Christian belief. I remember Mark saying to me, "Did you feel the same way when your husband died?" He could not believe that God would let his wife die just like that. His problems ranged from sleeplessness to restlessness. Fear of new relationships and the fear that he would not be a competent father overtook him. I told Mark not to doubt the power of God. Sometimes it is hard to explain to someone in pain that things will get better. The question of "Why me?" will always be asked. It is not easy to understand why these things happen. We must also understand that being Christians does not exonerate us from problems of this world. In fact, Christians are more prone to problems because the devil attacks God's children faster and more often than anyone else.

About six months later, I met Mark at a funeral service. A young man had died from a brief illness. Mark asked me if I would ever marry again. I told him that I would not marry again but asked why? He did not respond. I was a little concerned about his reaction. I wanted to know what was wrong. I knew something was going on in his mind. He explained that he knew he would marry again, but he was not comfortable with his thoughts and did not know what to do. I found out that Mark was living in the fear of his wife's death. Could he ever marry again? What if this second one died too? He needed to hear from me and maybe a few other people how they feel about losing their spouses. I always prayed for Mark. I gave him a few books and tracts about death and dying given to me by friends and well-wishers.

I had nothing more to offer Mark than prayers, which did not seem to be enough at that time, but that of course was what he needed. I told him to continue to pray and to look up to God. I knew he was a Christian and I reminded him to continue in upholding his faith in God. I told him to lay down his burden at God's feet. I gave him one of my favorite verses in the Bible and thought that it was appropriate for his situation. He has to trust God and let Him take control of his feeling and decisions.

Proverbs 3:5,
Trust in the Lord with all thine heart;
And lean not unto thine own understanding.
In all thy ways acknowledge him,
And he shall direct thy paths.

I prayed this every day of my life. I asked God to guide me and not allow me to take things into my hands or take anything for granted. No matter what our feeling may be, we must not forget to let Christ direct our thoughts and our ways. The moment we let Him control our desires, our thoughts will be focused on the things that delight Him. Our lives will change, and the things of this world will go strangely dim in the light of His glory and grace. Mark had the need to remarry, but had not the courage to face it. He needed someone outside of his family, someone he could trust, or perhaps some Christian from his church or a friend to let him know that it is appropriate and on time. He simply needed support. I prayed that God would send him a Christian wife, one he would cherish for the rest of his life. People need each other in times like these. I was saved by prayers from good people and I promised that I will be of service to others too.

John had to live with grandmother for a short time. Mark would always say that life was not fair. He repeatedly cried, "It is not fair, it is not fair at all." He was angry at death and was frustrated with life. He wished he could have stopped his wife's death. Life was not fair. Although Mark was devastated about his wife's death, he soon started dating. He knew that he would not mourn forever and that life, of course, must continue. He was very skeptical about another relationship, but also was aware of the comfort he desired so he must seek for that. He needed someone to share his life with right away. A new relationship was like a necessity for him. There was no waiting. He remarried and now has four children, including John. Life is not fair yet life goes on.

Esther Lee:

Esther was young. She had just turned twenty-four years old when her husband of five years died in an automobile accident. Seth and Esther were high school classmates. Seth was twenty-six years old at his untimely death. Their marriage was blessed with two children, Alexia four years old and Andy two years old. What more could the devil do to a young couple? Seth had just started a new job. Things were going well with them. A devastating death could have been the last thing anyone could think of for these young people. When the news of his accident reached home, friends and family members were already there to comfort Esther. "No one could believe the story that Seth was gone," said Esther as she told me her ordeal. A friend to her mother had told her about me and wanted her to talk with me. I asked her what she was doing and how long ago her husband died.

She told me that it was barely nine months since her husband died and that she was home with her children. In asking, I found out that she had never worked in her life. She was about to go to college when she changed her mind and married her high school sweetheart. She told me that she had nothing to offer herself or her children. She had no desire for marriage anymore. She would like to go to college but did not know how or where to start. She would like to get a job but had no clue of how to hold a job and at the same time care for her children. As she told me everything, I saw an amazing strength in this young lady. She wanted to do everything possible to help herself, but could not. I asked her why she came to me, and she said that she did not know, but that her mother's friend had told her to go and talk to me. The person who sent her had told her that no matter what, that she would get some good advice from me.

I neither knew Esther nor the lady who sent her. She later explained to me that this lady was one of my clients. She gets her medications from my pharmacy and knew when my husband passed away.

Telling Esther to go home and pray was not going to be enough. She needed action. She needed to know that prayer would work for her. Esther was a Christian of the Catholic faith. She told me that she did not pray much and that she went to church only when she could. Her age, her needs, and her alacrity were really overwhelming for me. I am neither a counselor nor a preacher. I did not know what to do to help her. One thing I learned to do was to tell God my problems. Her problems became my problems. She only needed someone to advise her on what to do. She needed someone to comfort her and make her feel like somebody. She wanted to know that she could still make it in life. She had been told that she was now on her own since Seth died.

Life was not easy for Esther as a widow. Although she was young and pretty,

—Life had no meaning to her anymore.

—She saw herself as helpless and surrounded by enemies.

—Marriage was a thing of horror; she felt rejected by her husband's family.

—She had no self-esteem, because no one cared anyway.

—She had fear, anger, hate, frustration, resentment, and depression.

For several days I spoke with her, and the more we talked, the more she asked me questions:

What if I don't marry again?

Will I be able to take care of my children?

Will I be able to go back to school?

Why do people seem like they feel sorry for me and yet they act mean?

I was not able to answer all her questions but whatever, I could do, I did to help her. Several times, I talked with her over the telephone. I told her of my loss and how I have struggled to overcome all my fears. I realize that it was not easy for her, being much younger than I was, but I remembered what Mrs. Jenkins told me: "No time is best, at any age and time, give God glory, for you never know His will for you."

Esther went back to school and finished a college degree. She is able to care for her children. Five years later, she remarried and is happy with her family. It only took determination and trusting in God. Her fears were gone and her hope for a better life was fulfilled.

Ms. Sadie Cox:

Six years after Sadie emerged from a bitter divorce, she met her second husband, Andrew Cox. Between Sadie and Andy, there were seven children. Three boys and a girl from Sadie's previous marriage, and two boys and a girl came from Andy's first marriage. Amazingly, things were going on very well with this couple and they had no reason to complain. Sadie and Andy were financially well off and all the children were well taken care of.

I met Sadie at a graduation party for a friend's daughter. She had asked if the gentleman sitting next to me was my husband. I said no, I did not know who he was. She went on to say, "Are you by yourself?" I said no, "I came with my son," pointing to my son who was talking with his friends. She pulled her chair closer to mine and said, "Oh, I came alone, I did not know anyone here, can I sit and talk with you?" She said that she was a colleague of the host family.

As we talked, we found out that we had something in common. We were both widows. We exchanged phone numbers and wished each other well. I never thought that I would have reason to call Sadie again, but several weeks later, I started thinking about her. Thoughts of Sadie filled my heart each day. I knew she was very lonely, even at the party. I remembered how she asked if she could talk to me. She said to me that there was something about me that made her come closer to speak to me. As I thought about her, I wished I could call the number she gave me, but for some reason I could not come up to doing so.

I started to pray for Sadie. I just knew she was a widow and she was not very young and not very attractive either. Sometimes I would say to myself that I too have my own problems and did not need to worry or think about other people's problems. Why should I think about her so much? But I knew that Sadie needed me. But who am I that I should feel that way for her? It took about six months before I could make up my mind to call. God is great. Everything that happens in our lives has a reason and happens at the right time. I called Sadie.

She did not remember my name. She had lost my phone number apparently the same day I gave it to her. She had been praying that I would one day call her. She had prayed to God to send me her way again. When I introduced myself over the phone again, she could only remember the lady she met at that party and wished to see again. At this time, Sadie asked me for a visit. I was glad that she asked. Three days later, I went to her house in Los Angeles. She lived about thirty miles from me. It took about twenty-five minutes' drive inland to get to her. It was on a Sunday afternoon that I went and met Sadie.

She lived in a beautiful home in a nice neighborhood. She introduced her four children to me and showed me pictures that included her husband and three other children. I thought she expected me to say something about the pictures, but I did not. I was not going to make her say things unless she wanted to. She had already told me on the first day we met that she was a widow. As we sat down and watched the three young men and the young lady disappear to their rooms, I asked her, "What did your husband die of?" She looked at me, lifted the pictures and handed them over to me as if to say that I should look at them again. She paused and said, "They all perished in one automobile accident." I screamed in awe. With my right hand over my mouth, my head down, I could not believe what I heard. Before too long, we were both crying as though it had just happened. I wished I did not come to visit. I thought that my visit had just brought back those sad memories to her. I moved over to her and said again and again, *I am sorry.*

It was three months after this deadly accident that I met Sadie for the first time. The death of her loved ones was still very fresh in her heart. At this point in time, Sadie still lived in a daze. I asked her what made her come to me at the party. She answered, "You were the only one that looked at me and smiled in that place. I felt strange all the time until I saw you." I could not remember smiling at her. My willingness to talk with people made it seem like they were welcome before asking. In reality, Sadie was welcome with all my heart the time we first met. Yes, she continued, saying that the smile on my face and my acceptance of her made her feel very comfortable. Thanks to God. I too needed to feel comfortable even among strangers. I had been told a few times to smile, that life just isn't that bad. But many times too, I have been asked, "Why are you smiling?" when actually the last thing on my mind would be to smile. I realized that most of the times that I had been told that I was smiling were times that I had stopped to reminisce over God's love and mercy on me, whereas the times that I had been told to smile were times that I had deeply fallen into thoughts of "Why me and why not…" Sadie may have caught me at one of the moments of reminiscing.

She told me about her first marriage, which ended in a bitter divorce, and how she met Andy and they lived happily together until the day she will never forget in her life. Her story reminded me of the advertisement that said something about **"the thrill of success and the agony of defeat."** She had thrilled in the successful break away from a bad marriage. She became happily married again. Suddenly everything turned sour by a horrible accident that left her and her four children agonizing. She felt defeated in all her efforts and life's endeavor.

Although she had children and a family, Sadie needed more than people to survive. She needed Christ in her. She needed the comfort that comes from the Holy Spirit. She needed to know that God had not left her. The death of her husband and children was very devastating. It seemed like nothing could ever comfort her. When I listened to her, it reminded me of the Bible story of the woman of Ramah called Rachel.

Mathew 2:18
A voice was heard in Ramah,
Lamentation, weeping and great mourning,
Rachel weeping for her children,
Refusing to be comforted,
Because they are no more.

No one could comfort her over the brutal killing of her twin children, killed when King Herod ordered that every male child of age up to two years should be killed. He heard of the birth of Christ and so wanted to kill every baby and toddler in Bethlehem and in all the districts, to make sure that Christ was not allowed to live. Rachel could not be comforted by anyone. Like Rachel, Sadie needed the comfort of the Holy Spirits, divine comfort that comes only from Christ. She needed just to bring her problems to Christ, trusting and believing that there is hope for those who believe. She had a battle to fight and only Christ could win this battle for her.

Sadie's fears were quite within expectations:

—Fears of how people may look at her situation.
—Fears of what would happen to her and her remaining children.
—Angry at death itself.
—Angry at God for allowing such a calamity on her family.
—Angry at the law. She could not prosecute (as she may have wished) the drunk driver who killed her husband and children.
—She had resentment and lack of trust in everything or even people.
—She could not trust anybody, because friends had started failing her.
—She stopped going to church completely.
—She felt deserted and lonely and sometimes blamed herself for her problems.

We met quite a few times, and sometimes just to pray. Sometimes we prayed over the telephone. We discussed our problems. We encouraged each other. My strength geared up her strength, and soon Sadie started going to her church again. She needed friends or people she could trust. She needed someone who understood and who would not bring her down for her feelings. In times like these, the last thing you need is anyone to criticize you or irritate your feelings. I remembered several times when I was like Sadie. God sent His loving people around me to comfort me. I knew how it felt and what it meant to have someone by your side who really understands your feelings. A Christian does not have to experience adversity in order to be able to comfort someone else. Although I was always reaching out to her, I found strength in talking to Sadie about the goodness of God. I found out that my strength and courage grew stronger as I reached out to more people.

Sadie is working with a big firm in the city of Los Angeles as a legal assistant. All her children are grown.

We are both happy to have met each other, and we owe our friendship to the love of Jesus Christ who, seeing our needs, provided for us.

It was not just as easy as expected each time I had to meet with someone. Sometimes I am met with situations that I would describe as unbearable.

There is a saying that when it rains it pours. This statement is as true as it is said. Sometimes I am met with people who, no matter what you do or say, will not accept the fact that there should be hope, and that faith in Christ could deliver them from their ordeal. Sometimes, I equally wondered why some people should be allowed to suffer so much.

I have just mentioned some peculiar cases. There are many more pathetic examples of what people go through in this life. I have just focused on spousal loss and the effect it has on the other spouse. Although I did not mention it in the abstracts, some of my most difficult acquaintances were with those in marriages between people of different ethnic groups or religious faiths. Several times I realize that the lack of understanding of the beliefs and culture or tradition of the other spouse poses a big problem when things go wrong. By this, I mean that whether in divorce or in death, regardless of the level of comfort that existed before the tragedy, there is always a problem over what was done or is to be done right or wrong. This problem is a lot deeper if the cultural or traditional needs do not match.

Mr. Abraham

He lost his first wife following a brief illness. She had left him with two sons. He remarried to a woman with two children. She had been divorced two years earlier and they both had one child together, Isaac, giving them a total of five children. I had never met them before. It was a friend who told me about them. I was able to call and speak with

Mr. Abraham, an African American. I promised him my prayers. He was a company driver. His wife, Marlene, was of Spanish background and a school nurse by profession. Three years after Isaac was born, he was diagnosed with leukemia. Isaac did not make it. He died shortly after. One year later, in the summer of 2000, Marlene died of a brain aneurysm.

The sudden deaths of his wife and child were unbearable for Mr. Abraham. He could not cope with his fate. He had a stroke and ended up with a right side paralysis. I did not know about this until one year after his stroke, when a friend told me about it. At this time, he had regained some of the strength in his right hand. I called to say hello to him and to let him know that with faith in God, all will be well with him.

He was not friendly at first. When he demanded who I was and why I was calling, I told him who told me about his situation. He calmed down, took a deep breath and said, "Yes, I think I am fine."

Mr. Abraham repeated the story of his ordeal to me. He finally said, "I believe in God and I know that Christ had died for me, but see how helpless God has left me." He went on to say, "Life is not fair. Why would this happen to me? I cannot even take care of my children." Then he concluded by saying, "I thank God for friends and family, they have been of good help." Mr. Abraham had just finished blaming God for his condition and turned around to thank Him for other areas where things seem good. How could He be doing us evil and good at the same time? We should know that God is good to us all the time.

A ten-minute talk with Mr. Abraham told me that he was a Christian, or at least he knew about Christ. I reminded him of the story of Job in the Bible.

Job 14:1-2
"Man who is born of woman
Is of few days and full of trouble.

**He comes forth like a flower and fades away;
He flees like a shadow and does not continue."**

**Ecclesiastes 2:22-23
"For what has man for all his labor,
And for the striving of his heart
With which he has toiled under the sun?**

**For all his days are sorrowful,
And his work burdensome;
Even in the night his heart takes no rest.
This also is vanity."**

I told him about Job's sufferings and his faith in God. He was just quiet over the phone. I could not hear a sound from his end. When I finished talking, I heard a heavy sigh from him, followed by a weary voice saying, "Do I have to be like Job for God to know that I believe in Him?" Mr. Abraham did not have to be like Job, but the truth is that anyone could be Job anytime. We all are like Job in all our afflictions. No matter what we are going through, we must remember that there is only one way to overcome. That way is Christ our Savior. Unless we come to God through Christ, we will not see salvation. Job never gave up hope in God. Only through trusting, believing with hope and praying with faith shall we embrace freedom from the bondage of adversity.

It was so sad listening to him repeatedly telling his adversity, his fate in life, his trust in God, and how things have turned out for him. I told him the story about the family that perished in the airplane crash. I told him to stop blaming God, but instead praise Him for spearing his life so that his children will at least have a parent alive. He was very difficult to convince that God did not put this on him. As I was about to drop the phone, trying to conclude my mission, I heard him say, "If only you can understand what death is or what it means to lose loved ones."

I immediately realized that I did not fully introduce myself to him. I said to him, "Yes I know because I have been there." I told him about the sudden death of my husband and exactly two years later, the devil struck again; my older sister, who was my mentor, took ill and died. I told him that I had not been sick, but that I had once felt even worse than he did. He was able to tell me how sorry he was for me. "I did not need you to be sorry for me," I told him. "I just want you to know that there are more people out there that have been through things just like you. I want you to stop feeling sorry for yourself and stop blaming anyone or even God for your problems." I told him how I blamed God and asked Him questions. When I talked to other Christians and started praying right, God lifted me from my fears. I made it my duty to tell others to do the same. We are born into a world of sin, and the only way to get salvation from this predicament is by trusting and believing in God through Christ. You must start now to trust in God and pray with faith and He will fulfill your hopes and desires. Even in your afflictions, you will find out that God has been good to you in other areas.

Mr. Abraham said that he was a Christian who believed that he understood the will of God. He did not believe that he would suffer as he did. When problems came his way, his faith in God was found lacking. Most Christians these days are of weak faith. We say we trust in God and believe in Him, yet when problems come our way, we find out that we are lacking in faith and we start blaming Him. We do not know how to turn our problems over to God through Christ our Savior. Sometimes, we need someone to give us a push and remind us that there is an ever-ready help, Christ who laid his life that we may be saved.

There are times in our lives when we sit and ponder over some of our encounters and wonder what could have happened if things had happened the other way. Sometimes we wonder why some people, especially Christians, experience adversities over and over again. We wonder if God really loves us as He says in the Bible. Of course God knows and sees everything. We tend to forget about Satan, the devil. The devil is the advocate of all evils that befall man.

I could see why Mr. Abraham felt rejected by God. I myself could not imagine how I am able to tell someone to be still when I think of my experiences. It was not until I fully realized what it meant to have Christ in me that I began to understand fully the power of the Holy Spirit. It was only exactly two years after my husband passed away, I had just started to gain some courage and strength, my children and I were beginning to adjust to living without fear then tragedy struck again. I could say that I knew where Mr. Abraham was coming from.

My oldest sister, who was my mentor, a Christian evangelist, was snapped away by the wicked hands of death. Sister Peace as she was known, passed away after a brief illness following an acute renal failure. Her death was a big shock to our family. My mother, my siblings, my children, and every friend of hers and the family thought it was one of the most devastating of its kind. It was obvious that I should break down at this time. While I was worried for my mother, she too was praying strongly that God should give me courage to deal with it. My children wondered why their auntie should die just exactly two years following their father's death. I, in my own understanding, thought that the devil was against me. I could not understand why it had to be me again. As I grieved over my sister's death, so many thoughts ran through my mind. It was just like yesterday; I had two wonderful friends. These were my greatest mentors. Two people that I trusted and thought that nothing will ever happen to me as long as they were praying for me. Now I could look around everywhere and search and call, and they would not be there nor even answer. My husband and my sister were gone. The strange part of this is that these two were devoted Christians. They both loved people and stood out in life for their families and friends, regardless of circumstances. I did not think that life had any meaning, neither did God make sense to me anymore. It made sense then to ask, **"Why me?"**

When situations get this tough, people—even Christians—become tempted to denounce religion, Christianity, God, and everything about Him. I asked and wanted to know if God discriminates, or why would it be me again? Although I wished I could, I did not stop attending church services. I could not disappoint my children or lead them astray. I realized that whatever I said or did at that time would abound. I believe that the Holy Spirit was with me and kept me going. I had a job to do for my Maker. I had to teach and direct my children. I know that my mother and my sibling were worried about me, and I had to show some strength and support for their own feelings too. It was hard to see face-to-face with God. We were just two months old in our new church when it happened. A few months later, during the revival evangelism, my eyes were opened when I heard the preacher saying those magical words, **"In every adversity, God plants a seed of equal or greater benefit."** I knew right away that God has something for me. I only had to pick up courage and trust in Him.

It has become my sincere heart's desire to tell everyone this same good news. It does not matter how happy you think you may be. We have all sinned and come short of the glory of God. We are all subject to adversities. Problems will come from everywhere. The devil plans and proposes, but we must allow the spirit of holiness to abide in us, so that Christ, who is our Savior will be the one to dispose. He will not dispose the plan of the devil on us. He will dispose for us the will of His father, God our Heavenly Father.

I have seen and heard all kinds of problems from both young and old and all walks of life. From death of any kind to the littlest form of abuse or affliction, all seen as the adversities that plagues this world today. Death especially sudden death of no origin is the most devastating.

Death is an inevitable end of this mortal life. It is the devil's abuse to God's children. It originated from sin. The loss of a loved one makes us to sorrow for what we cannot help. It brings us to a level of acceptance with things we cannot control. One thing we should never sit and wonder or worry about is death. According to the Bible, it is there and will happen because this mortal flesh must die. Regardless of what our adversity may be, we have been asked to give it all to God in prayer through Christ our savior.

Amelia

This woman who I call a friend of mine today, is a humble God-loving young lady. She is the kind of woman you will not hesitate to call a true Christian. She would call on God for everything. She is a true believer. Amelia is married to a non-believer. At the time of their marriage, her husband had purported to be a Christian. Of course, everyone says, *I am a Christian,* either because their parents were Christians or they were baptized in early childhood in Christian churches as chosen by their parents or guardians. Most of these people grow up not knowing what it means to accept Christ as their personal Savior. Several men and women face this heartbreaking problem in their marriages. It may come from either spouse. Such is the fate of my friend, Amelia. I have come across more women than men in this predicament. Some had married dangerous people without knowing it. In fact, in all my encounters, talking to people who are hurt for one reason or another, I have only come across a handful of men with unbelieving wives. Usually there are more women battling with unbelieving husbands.

Some spouses refuse to understand that there is a Supreme Being, God, who is the author and finisher of all lives. Every marriage should be based on His principles of the union. Most men recite the statement that the man is the head of the family, but they also forget that the head has a duty to coordinate with the subordinates, (the rest of the body). Since society has made it such that women are equally breadwinners for families, people no longer view it as a serious offense or a sin when a man is not able to provide for his family. The female spouse may have a better job than the male spouse. Sometimes this may deprive the man of his rights to be the spokesperson of the home. He may still try to impose that leadership ability on his family. The problem here is "impose." Things get out of hand when they are not settled amicably.

Amelia, like most other women, had the problem of a spouse who did not know Christ. He refused to acknowledge that there is a God. He did not want anyone to mention Christ or God around him. In his inability to provide for their three children and his wife, he was not tamed with words or behavior either. Although he drank randomly and had no problem controlling his drinking habits, he had his ways with women. This did not leave him with much money in his pockets. Whenever he was home, it was hell house for the entire family. When he stopped going to church, he told his wife and child that the more they prayed and went to church, the more the devil will attack them. He would not pray, and would blame his inability to provide for the family on the fact that his family believed in God. He finally lost his job. He was allowed to live in his house as the head of the family and as he wished. He did not at any time try to reduce his spending habits. He would collect money from his wife to satisfy his women friends, and buy his drinks.

Amelia lived in fear. She was lonesome, angry, and frustrated. When I spoke with her, she told me that she wished she was never married, but would not think of divorce. She said that she was always afraid of what he was going to do next whenever he came home. She understood the Bible and she knew that the path of her marriage was not going to be easy. She was all ready to hand over her problems to God. Amelia was one of those who would not hesitate to ask someone for help, although she loved to keep certain things to herself. I started praying together with Amelia. She was strong in her faith. Once in a while, she would break down and cry. After listening to her narrating her problems, I wondered why she was still in the relationship. I asked, "What if things don't improve?" She said, "Then God will make a way for me and my children." I thought that this lady was amazing. In her fears and pains, she was very strong and completely believed that she would overcome in the name of Jesus Christ. She is just one out of several men and women who would dare the devil in their marriages, believing that if God did not want them in that relationship, He would make a way out for them.

Sometimes, as we get submerged in our thoughts and problems, we tend to forget what we already believe in. We ponder around and wonder what could be done to make things right. God sends someone our way to remind us that He is still in charge. I may have thought or it may seem that I was helping Amelia out of her problems, whereas she was at this time even making me stronger in my own faith. Her faith that God will vindicate her made me stronger each day as I prayed with her. We both believed that God has a purpose for her in that relationship.

When Amelia came to me, she had in mind that I was a prayerful person and that I could understand her problems and pray with her. Of course, she was right. What she did not know was that she too was a very strong prayer warrior.

Her courage was amazing, but she had allowed the influence of an unbelieving husband to put her down. The more I met with her, the better I felt and the more I realized how God can use His children to strengthen one another. She exercised great faith in God. Although her marriage has not become one of the greatest, she has been able to bring her husband to understand the need for prayer and believing in God. I always thank God for the people He sends my way.

Grandma Cecilia

I would not forget the plight of Ms. Cecilia, a Christian grandmother and a faithful believer. Ms Cecilia was a seventy-two-year-old great-grandmother when I met her. She had come to my pharmacy to pick up a prescription for a little six-month-old child. She asked me to explain to her again how to give the medications. She was picking up four different medications for cough, cold, pain, and infection. After I had explained everything to her, she left the bag of medications on the counter and sort of angrily stormed out of the pharmacy. She came back within minutes with an elderly man whom she introduced as her husband. She asked me to please tell them everything over again. I was not offended. I knew there was a problem somewhere or maybe they both needed to hear me together.

Ms. Cecilia was busy collecting the medicine and talking sweetly to the baby in her hand, saying, "Here, baby, I got this for you, and you are going to be well soon."

I asked about the baby's Parents.

The old man turned to me and started a conversation. He tried to avoid my question and then quickly said, "I do not mean to neglect your question, you asked for his parents, eh?" I answered, "Yes, are they at work?" Both grandparents said simultaneously, "I wish." Ms. Cecilia then told me that their granddaughter was the baby's mother. She said that his father was a "nobody." She said, "I will not give him

114

away to nobody." About two hours later, the phone rang and I was told that it was the lady with the baby, as she described herself. She wanted to know again how to give the medicines. After I explained to her again, she asked me which one of them she was supposed to refrigerate. I told her the pink one, but if you forget to do so, it is not a problem. She thanked me and said that she was happy that I was not offended by her many questions.

The next day, Ms Cecilia called and told me that she did not want to go back to the hospital with the baby. She would rather talk to me because she thinks that I am a Christian too. The baby was still ill. He was not getting any better. I told her to continue on the medicines for at least five days. I assured her that the baby would be well. I did not hear from her again for several months.

In July of 1997, Ms. Cecilia showed up at my pharmacy again with a handsome little toddler and said, "Do you remember me and my baby?" "Of course I do, we all here do remember you," I replied. "She said that she had come to tell us why she stopped at my pharmacy several months ago. On that day as we were going home I saw the name NEW HOPE PHARMACY, and I decided to come in here. I thought that God had something to tell me. I was going home to the pharmacies in my neighborhood. My husband and I had been to Harbor UCLA hospital all day. I was going home to kill myself. My husband and I had gotten to a point of no turning back from our fights. When we came here, regardless of my nagging, you and your staff were kind to us. That day, we traveled home in peace after you gave us the medications. My hope was renewed after my trip to your New Hope. This baby," she said, "is the bone of contention between me and my husband. His mother is our granddaughter, our baby grandchild to be exact. Her mother, our daughter, died of cancer three years before this baby was born. We took care of my granddaughter, who was fifteen years old when her mother died. We did not know about her bad group of friends until it was too late. She was already pregnant. She did not listen to us. She was killed shortly after the baby was born. Her boyfriend, the baby's father is a nobody. My husband wanted to give this baby up for adoption. I would not live to see that happen. This child is doing very well. If I could do anything for my daughter and my grandchild, it will be to care for 'my baby' as she called him. I have two problems that I am dealing with… My husband does not want the child. He says that we are too old to do this. Secondly, this child looks like his father, and I am not able to forgive him for the death of my granddaughter."

It was hard for her to live with the same face that brought her adversity. She told me that she needed my prayers. " I know you are a Christian, I know you can pray, just pray for me." She finally said that she just wanted to stop by and thank me for all my help.

We can again see that Ms. Cecilia was dealing with multiple issues and the problems that come with adversities. We may not seem to comprehend the things that go on in the minds of the afflicted. Here is an old woman who has lived her life and probably so well. At her age, problems would still surface that could tie her down on her feet again, raising a little baby orphan. There is reason and purpose for everything. Take every problem with a grain of salt and bring it to the Lord in prayers.

She battled with:

—The death of her daughter from cancer.

—The death of her baby granddaughter (gang issue).

—Non-compliance from her husband over the baby's welfare.

—The anger of what comes to her mind when she sees the very baby she wants to hold and keep.

—The frustration that comes with caring for a baby at her age.

I often called her to ask about the baby. Her husband mellowed down and became receptive of their great-grandchild as he grew older. This was something they would have to deal with for the rest of their lives. They could not forget their daughter or their granddaughter, but sure enough can forgive the father of their great-grandbaby and continue with their lives and the good work they were already doing. I told them about **God's seed of equal or greater benefit.** God never fails. He knows how and when to reward us for our steadfast trust in Him. I told them not to be afraid of what they cannot do but to remember that if they believed in Christ as they said, they could always do all things regardless of their age, especially if they put their mind in it and for a good course. Going back to scripture, she would always say it before I did, **Philippians 4:13, "I can do all things through Christ who strengthens me."**

Sometimes in one's life, things go wrong. Everything would seem to stand still or turn upside down. Friends and even family may turn against you. It may be for your belief or for inevitable circumstances, just remember that you cannot give up hope at any time. Friends and family told them to give up that child for adoption, but she strongly believed that God needed her to care for that child and she held onto her belief. She never regretted what she believed in.

Where there is life, there must be hope. Hope is only for the living and not for the dead. Because they knew their scriptures and knew that God was there for them, their hurt could not destroy their faith. They had lived their lives together for fifty-three years, retired and in good health. Then tragedy struck, one after the other, leaving them with an infant to care for. Ms. Cecelia's faith was strong and I found strength in her too.

I visited her home only once and it was a bittersweet occasion. Following her questions, I told her how I became a widow and much about my family. She asked about my business and why I do not open on Sabbath days. I asked if she meant Saturdays. She said yes but again said Sabbath. I smiled and said, "Because I am an Adventist." Both she and her husband screamed, "I knew it, I knew it!" I found out that we were of the same faith. We cried and prayed together. Her husband then introduced himself for the first time as Andrew Hickenson. Surprisingly, Mr. Hickenson became very open and praised God for His infinite mercy. He brought out his own Bible and read with us from the scripture:

Revelation 21:4
And God shall wipe away all tears from our eyes;
And there shall be no more death,
Neither sorrow, nor crying,
Neither shall there be any more pain:
For the former things are passed away.

It is always a joy to know that these things shall come to pass and that God's promises are numerous and not vain. He shall wipe away all tears from our eyes. All the troubles of the earth will one day pass away. It touched my heart when we read this scripture, because it was one of my husband's favorite scriptures and we sang it occasionally during our devotions. He was very pleased to teach our children that song when he was alive.

Ms. Cecilia's baby was later sent to his aunt at the age of five to start school. His aunt lives in the South. I understand that the Hickensons later moved down South too to spend the rest of their lives with family and old friends. Thanks to God for friends and family, those who step in when help is eminent. Meeting these people and being a part of their testimonies have strengthened my life and has continued to help me in reaching out to others.

What about wiping away all tears from our hearts? We should never attempt being angry with God. His will is always best for us, and that's why it is necessary that we pray to Him, saying: **Thy will be done, on earth as it is in heaven**. We should start praying for our will to be His will too.

Several months after my husband passed away, my younger sister was to get married. It was a happy occasion, although we were all touched by the fact that he was not there to witness the very occasion he prayed so much for. After the wedding, we still often talked about the fact that strangely enough, he was no more.

One morning, my sister called me. I knew that she was expecting a baby and that the due date was near. She was very hesitant to say why she had called. "I don't know how I feel or how you may feel about this," she said. "Okay, what is it?" I said. She pursed, sighed, and finally said, "The baby is expected on February 27th." I was about to ask if that was a problem for her when it dawned on me, February 27th. It was exactly two years ago, February 27th, that my husband passed away. I heard myself screaming lowly, "O my God, no! no! no! that is not right, we must pray. That's not the right date."

I could not accept that day to be a birthday in the family. It had been set aside as my day to mourn and question God. Regardless of the fact that I had accepted in faith the passing of my husband, I still found myself at this moment believing that I must mourn all my life. If God wills it, so be it.

A handsome bouncing baby boy was born on February 27, 1996. God gave me a break. If anyone tells otherwise of God, that person is not real. In my prayers, I had always asked God to deliver me from the adversity of death. I did not want to live with that date as a day of anguish for the rest of my life. When He was about to answer my prayers, I started running from it. He is a mighty God and He answered anyway. This might have been a coincidence, but I saw it as one of the ways God wipes away our tears and tells us that we could not mourn like we have no hope. At that time, I did not realize what He was doing for me. He had to prepare me for the greater things that I will encounter and rejoice in.

My little nephew, whose name means "the will of God," now makes my day every February 27th of each year. He starts from weeks before till days before until that very day calling and reminding me that his birthday is coming. If there is anything to be done on the morning of every February 27th, it has to be the singing of "Happy Birthday" to an innocent child. He must always make sure that I take care of that day for him. That day is no more a day of sorrow for me.

We do not forget what happened, but God has wiped away all tears from our eyes. The birth of a little child would have disciplined us to the will of God. Rejoice and be glad in Him because there is hope for reunion with all our loved ones in heaven.

CHAPTER EIGHT

Discipline in Times Like These

It is always easy to focus on adults and their feelings when tragedy strikes. Adults seem to react to these situations faster or in a more profound way. Children have feelings too. In fact, it is very important to look closely to their reaction immediately and continuously whenever things don't seem right in any family. It is important to discipline everyone to understand the situation at hand. Every member's feelings must be accommodated. I want to remind my readers again that I am not a certified counselor. I am not a preacher, nor am I a Bible teacher. I am a Christian, a mother of four wonderful children, a widow, and I am using my experiences to enrich other people. In times of sorrow, as in times of joy, we are asked to be disciplined in our teachings. Do not mourn like you have no hope. Do not get drunk by your happiness. Discipline helps us understand God's will for us. We must be willing to accept this discipline. My encounters are not out of the ordinary. The way I faced my problems is not out of the ordinary. I believe that by reaching out to many people who may have a chance to read this book, I am fulfilling my purpose in life. I am doing what I am supposed to do, which is to let others know that there is nothing that will happen to you at any time in your life that you and your Heavenly Father cannot take care of. There is reason for everything. No burden is too heavy to carry if you believe in God through Christ our Savior. I asked God to allow His Holy Spirit to discipline my ways with my children. I was not willing to spare the rod and lose my children. **Proverbs 13:24**. We needed him to lead and discipline us in his just way. Lead us not into temptation dear Lord, but deliver us from the works of evil people.

It is said that the worst thing that could happen to a parent is to have a bad child. By the same token, the worst thing that could happen to a child is to have a bad parent. Children do worry about parents as parents worry about them. I know exactly how my children reacted towards their father's death. I was watching them and I realized that they too were watching me. The pains I went through also were their problem. I know that this is the same with most families where there is the love of God. They all worried about my safety maybe even more than I worried about theirs. God blessed us with wonderful children and I wanted to be a good parent to them too.

Three days after my husband passed away, my oldest child, who was sixteen years old at that time, decided that she must go and get her driver's license. She was anxious and was undoubtedly very worried. She said that she would not want Mommy to drive. I told her that even if she got her license that day, it would not make her my safe driver. She decided that whatever the case may be, I was not allowed to drive. She thought that my disposition at that time was not safe enough to let me drive.

Whenever we finished our devotion at night—this usually took place downstairs in the family room—I would stand at the foot of the staircase and watch them all walk up the stairs to their bedrooms. A few months later, my older son would say, "Mommy, go. I will be the last one to go upstairs. I am the man of the house, I am fourteen years old now." We would all laugh. I asked him one day why he thought he would be the one watching over us as we walked upstairs. He said that since Daddy was not there, he was the next oldest male in the house. My heart was touched by his statement. I love him for his concern, but that night was very rough for me. I cried to God and asked him why he had allowed my young son to become the man of the house. It was one of those nights of **"why me."** It is one thing for us adults to cry and wish that we did not have to go through so much in our afflictions; but how about the other, being able to imagine what goes through the hearts of little children when they have to take up adult responsibilities because of adversities?

Isaiah 54: 17

No weapon that is formed against thee shall prosper:
And every tongue that shall rise against thee in judgment thou shall condemn.

I would speak these words like they were meant for me. I believe in God and I said strongly and always, "We will not die." This scripture tells me that God is my shelter and defender. It was not just my children who were afraid of my disposition. I always watched them in their sleep. I would always sneak into their rooms and come so close to make sure that everyone was breathing. I would panic at every complaint they made, no headache or stomach ache was simple to me. It had to be taken care of. I was afraid of death. As I feared almost everything, I used the scripture above to rebuke the devil and evil men. Nothing can rise against me as long as I believe and trust in God. He will condemn all those who speak evil against me. He is my father.

The first time I went out after their father's death, it was not easy on me. It was to a wedding that my children found out that I was invited to, and they insisted that I should go. When I dressed up to go, they lined up by the staircase, singing, "Go Mommy, go Mommy." I asked them why they were so excited, and they told me that they were happy to see that I could still dress up and look good. Children would always care in their own little way. They worried about me just as I worried about them. The Lord really had His hands on us and disciplined us to love one another in Christ – even without our knowing it.

One day, they rented a movie and invited me to sit down and watch it with them. They knew that I did not care much about movies. When I refused and asked why, they told me that they just wanted me to sit with them as a family and we can watch it together, just as we do our prayers together. Children always know how to get their parents. They had planned this with my sister. I agreed, but told them that I would join them a little later. I could hear them laughing and calling me to come on. I came down the steps into the family room and just about to make a turn into the kitchen and continue with my chores, when I took a glance at the television in the family room and saw Mrs. Doubtfire pulling up his brassiere and his breasts sagging down. I yelled out, "What is that?" We were all laughing and my children were all jumping and screaming happily saying, "Yeh, yeh, Mommy is laughing." They told me that I had not laughed since Daddy died.

My sons would always ask to go on errands or places with me, and when I asked why, they would tell me that they wanted to make sure that no one touched me or made me mad for any reason. It is amazing to know what goes on in the minds of children when tragedies strike a family. We should not underrate them or neglect their feelings. Everyone suffers just like everyone else. Nothing should be taken for granted.

My oldest child turned seventeen years old and went to the university. We missed her so much. She had become my best friend at this time and always seemed to know what everyone needed. She reminded me of my oldest sister being there for us, her siblings. She was a true big sister to her siblings. To me, she was the friend I needed at that time. With her around, I felt secure about my business with the rest of the children. I remember her fears after her father died as she asked me if she would ever go to the university of her choice. She had visited this school of her choice with her father the year before, and they both liked it. I told her that we have to pray hard for admission to the school of her choice. As the letters of admission came in, we read and discarded them one by one. We had decided on a second choice when she called me at work one day; in the background, everyone in the house was rejoicing and struggling to speak into the phone at the same time.

I asked what was going on and they all broke the news. She had been admitted into one of the top schools in the nation. That was a mighty prayer answered. God allowed the admission, He would also provide for the education and it happened. I began to realize that God, of course, has His ways of answering our prayers. Subsequently, my second child attended the same university. My third and my fourth children equally attended other top-ranked universities in the nation.

The day after she left for the university, I noticed some notes all over the house. The kitchen walls, the refrigerator door, and the walls of their rooms all had notes on them. She had put up signs for them to remember the days to take out trash. She reminded them that they had to do their chores to make things easy for me. She even told them the consequences of not doing their chores. If they did not do the dishes, they would not have their choice of food, because Mommy would only give them "foo foo," an African dish which is easy to fix simply because the soup would already have been made and stored in the refrigerator. There was not much cooking needed. Mommy should not be left to wash dishes and cook food too.

Inside their rooms, she warned them to be nice to Mommy so that she would not cry. These children cared and worried about me. She called from school as often as possible and we would pray and cry together. There was a strong tie that held my family together, and that is and will always be **"PRAYER, faithful PRAYER."** This is what I call discipline.

I had to reassure my children that I would always be there for them. When they picked up courage and asked, I told them that I would not marry again. They would always remain my responsibility, and I was not going to leave them alone. I was very concerned about my sons especially my older son. After speaking with him one day, I gave him my assurance that I was never going to leave them alone and that I will try my best for them. He told me some of his fears, and wanted to know if we could make it without Daddy. I told him that God would take care of us. It is hard to really know what these children understood of death. One thing I know is that we never stopped praying. Some ill-fated people had told them that our house would be sold and that we would have to sell our cars and rent an apartment to live in. Some even said to their hearing that the best thing for their mother was to find another husband. I knew that some of their fears were based on all these stories from some miserable comforters. But God gave us all the courage to survive their wishful thought.

Believing that God has a reason for allowing me to become a single parent, I sought His help to make me a dedicated one. If He is the father to the fatherless, He then is equally the husband to the widow with these children. It was my belief and dedication to work for Him and to try my best and raise some worthy citizens that brought me this far. You ask me how I did it? I would proudly say at this point in time, "Faithful prayer, dedication, and trust in God through Christ my Lord and Savior." But all these could not happen without self-discipline. Submitting myself totally to God and asking Him to order all my steps and to discipline me in words and works made my ordeal less stressful. It was easy for me to discipline my children knowing that the Lord has equally discipline me.

What you just read is to say a few of the many fears that may be throbbing in a child's heart in times of uncertainty. When there is peace at home and tragedy comes, everyone wonders why our peace had to be disturbed. There is always the fear of what follows or what will happen next. For the things we cannot control, there is always a solution and that is to hand it over to the one that knows about it most. We have to understand the will and ways of God. He will not wish that evil should come our way. He will not wish that we should die. In fact, God wants us to live and be happy forever. He blesses us in everything. It is hard to explain these things to children. Oftentimes, adults find it difficult to comprehend the things of this world because we do not know how to act or what to do in the face of adversity. Children find it harder because they look up to us adults for answers. If they cannot find support in our eyes or our ways, they start losing faith in us, even in God Himself. We need to understand and know God and His will for us. When we understand who He is and what He wants us to do, then we will be able to help the little ones around us and even the older ones that are weak in their faith.

In speaking with several children whose parent or parents have passed away, I found out that just as the adults have their fears, so do the children. While one child wondered how Mom would make it, another wondered how Dad would make it. In situations where both parents are gone, the next adult figure closest to the family would have to play a big role in their lives. It becomes more devastating when these adult figures fail in their duty. Children look up to adults whether or not they are their parent. Those who fail them, especially orphans, have failed our Heavenly Father. Remember **Matthew 19:14: "But Jesus said, suffer little children, and forbid them not, to come unto me: for of**

such is the kingdom of heaven." We have equally been told to accept these children in order to see the kingdom of heaven. Anyone who would do otherwise would answer to his shame. When we are disciplined in the Lord, the children in our care will be taught in the fear of God.

I know that there are many other people, men and women and even children, who are going through so much and maybe even worse situations. I tell you all out there, do not hide and die in ignorance. The moment you realize that God is still in control of your daily life and that no person or weapon formed against you will prosper, you will begin to function right and without fear. You must reach out and say something to someone. Through prayer and relationships with other Children of God, I began to realize that some of my pains are unnecessary and without course. I realized that the worst thing in any adversity is fear, especially the fear of man. The fear of what man would say, the fears of what man would do, the fear of disappointing someone, or maybe the fear of disappointing oneself. If in any reason we should have fear, it should be the fear of not knowing God's will or not obeying the will we know.

We must ask God to discipline us in times of adversity. Discipline brings us to submission, obedience, faithfulness, and eventually drives away our fears of the enemy.

"Fear is the destruction that results from adversity. Discipline is to submit oneself completely to God." Your greatest sacrifice to God is your total surrender of self to Him, and this is the only way you can conquer fear. If I had to live the kind of life that I asked God for, I must then discipline myself to God's standard for my needs. I must learn to pray right and be constant and consistent in my prayers. I must build a better relationship with God. Through the help of a dear friend, a woman of grace, someone who had walked with God, I learned the secret of how to love God. She gave me books on God's love for His Children. I learned that in order for me to be happy, I not only should let go some of the anger in me, but I must also know and love myself. I must first discipline myself to God's love in order to discipline my children too.

If you want to be happy, you must be able to make someone happy. You cannot make someone happy if you have anger in you. If you love yourself, you will surely be happy with yourself. The joy you have in you reflects on your reactions with other people. This goes back to the great commandment, **"Love your neighbor as yourself."** I needed to be disciplined to be able to pray right and to find God's favor. Where there is love, there should be no fear of the enemy. Adults and children must all be disciplined alike for the family to function as one and in the fear of God. It was very important for me to be disciplined in all my ways in order to be able to teach my children right.

Marthew 10:28
Fear not them which kill the body,
But are not able to kill the soul .....

The soul belongs to God, and He alone can kill the body and the soul. Why should I be afraid of man or things of this world? A few hours after my husband passed away, events that took place immediately reminded me that as far as this world was concerned, I was alone. I was going to run my race alone. I knew that I had family and friends, but there were limits to what other people can do for me at this time. I knew that I had to be strong. I was not going to let my emotions or people's emotions direct my ways. People had other priorities as to what they wanted of me than what needed to be done. I knew that I had a strong battle to fight, keeping friends and family members together and on a suiting level. Finding who would really understand my feelings was not easy. This, in fact, was not to mention of those who thought that my children and I would be a burden on them. It seemed that we became a burden even before we could ask for help. Close friends and family may sometimes say or do things that would make you believe that you had become a burden on them. Do not be discouraged, but continued to ask God not to allow the enemy to encroach in your life or the lives of your children.

In every adversity, while some people are busy praying for your comfort, others would be busy counting your blessings and comparing it with your misfortune. They may rejoice over it or they may recount it to you as though you were being reminded that you had been doomed forever. Although some well-meaning friends and family may be there for you, because of human error, most well-meaning comments and reactions may turn sour. This most often triggers a pressure that immediately defeats the other good things around. This is the time you need to pray for God's never failing relationship. I asked Him to show me the right people and help me chose wise relationships that I may not go astray or allow negative emotions to overtake my life.

The devil would always attack God's people in our weakest dispositions through the ill-fated people and would instill the spirit of fear in our minds to destroy us. We should not allow the defeat of the evil one. We must learn that God does not want us to be afraid in times like this. He promised to be with us and He would not fail us. When we Christians surround ourselves with things about God, we must know that the devil would surely have no power over us. This portion of this book will bring us to know that fear can destroy every part of us to make us more vulnerable in our adversity. Only the Grace of God will deliver us from it. Do not give in to fear. Learn from other people's experiences and be prepared in case of emergency.

The apostle Paul tells us in the book of **2 Timothy Chapter 1:7—**

For God hath not given us the spirit of fear, but of power, and of love, and of sound mind.

God gave us the power to overcome the devil. He gave us the spirit of love, which brings us the peace of mind we need. He gave us the spirit of sound mind, which brings us self-discipline and better understanding. I needed to discipline myself and accept God's promises. I needed to give back to God just a little bit of myself by heeding His words.

The concept of fear varied in different individuals I came in contact with, depending on their adversity. I was very inquisitive, just to find out if anyone felt the same way I did. I realized that fear is not just a common thing but also a serious threat in people's lives. So as time passed by, I began to gradually test my willingness to live as I prayed. I was not going to allow what people said or did to stop me from being who I want to be. There is a saying that the man who knows the path of his enemy will always rule the enemy. I was so overwhelmed with fear that I was afraid of fear itself. I could not see the path of fear, which had sort of become a part of me. I wondered how well God heard my prayers or if He knew that I was afraid of something. It was an unexplainable fear. Several years later, I found out that I was not alone. There is a certain kind of fear that overtakes us when there is adversity. In reality, this fear is unexcused, yet we all go through its torture when we have no reason to.

Fear is the enemy of all occasions. It is described as an unpleasant, often strong emotion, caused by expectation or awareness of danger. Fear interferes with our hopes and defeats our purpose for life. As an enemy of all occasions, fear can step into our minds in times of danger to destroy every hope of encouragement. It also may step into our hearts in times of abundance and destroys all hopes of continuous joy in Christ. Fear destroys relationships and creates enmity between God's children.

Fear destroys life and puts people in bondage. Several good works have been destroyed by fear.

Such is the story of Adam and Eve as seen in the book of **Genesis chapter 3**. Man, as God's favorite creation, was brought down by the serpent in the Garden of Eden because of fear. This is the fear brought about by greed. Satan did not want Adam and Eve to be obedient to God. Satan feared the rule of God over God's own creation. He was in a self-imposed competition with God. Adam and Eve, in turn, were afraid of what they would lose if they did not obey the liar, Satan. Once they obeyed the devil, Adam and Eve then started to hide from God for fear of consequences of their sin. Fear has been hunting man from time immemorial. It is the same fear that brought a brother against his brother, Cain and Abel. These things still happen on earth today, the fear brought about by greed or jealousy.

Sometimes we forget the thrill that follows success and settle with the fear of success. Fear defeats success. We are so afraid of what would happen if... We settle with less. On the other hand, the agony and fear of defeat sometimes pushes us to gear up effort and do better or it may also make us to shy away from an imminent success and settle for defeat. We should not be slaves to fear. It is an enemy and we are supposed to fight it. Several times, I was faced with fear and uncertainty, and oftentimes thought that things have really come to a standstill. I would turn to my hymnals, searching for the right song to sing to suit my feelings. I would turn to my Bible for words of comfort and the right prayer verses. I wondered why oftentimes I would do all that I know to do, but my fear would still linger. Not until I realized who my enemy was did I see the light of God's love and promises for my family. God has not given us the spirit of fear. That is to say that the fear of the enemy is not of God. I was supposed to be strong in my faith and stand before the enemy and rebuke him.

During such times of fear, I would sing aloud, songs of praise; telling God that I know He is there and that I am counting on Him. One such song was my father's favorite song, "Give to the Winds thy Fears." This song is also based on the scripture found in the book of **Psalms 37:4... "Commit thy way unto the Lord; Trust also in him; and he shall bring it to pass."**

English	Igbo
Give to the winds your fears;	Gi atula egwu:
In hope be undismayed;	Nel'anya Chineke,
God hears your sighs and counts your tears,	O nuwo is'ude I n'akwa I,
God shall lift up your head.	O g'ebul'isi gi.
Through waves, and clouds, and storms	N'ime nsogbu nk'uwa
He gently clears thy way:	O n'akwara I uzo;
Wait thou His time; so shall this night	Chere mgbe Ya, abali nka
Soon end in joyous day.	G'ebi n'ubochi onu.

Just singing the first two verses, especially in the language I speak best, Igbo, brings courage and strength to my soul. This is a very powerful weapon in prayer. The thought that someone bigger and stronger than I am, Christ our Lord, would take my fears and problems away, made me feel like an eagle with great wings. I felt like I could fly and fly away to freedom as I sang my song.

As years went by and as I came in contact with more and more people who had suffered one kind of adversity or the other, I began to realize that we all suffered one common affliction. Everyone at one point in time, regardless of their situation, suffers some kind of siege of fear. You would hear people saying, "My fear was that so and so…" or "I was afraid of so and so." It seems like fear was the only problem we have. Without fear, man would move mountains, be completely hopeful, faithful, and trusting. Our fear of tomorrow is our enemy.

Fear is of two kinds. One is the fear of God and the second fear is the fear of man or circumstances. The fear of God, which is said to be the beginning of wisdom, is the fear in reverence to God as our Heavenly Father. We should be apprehensive or be afraid of God. To fear God is to obey Him and be faithful to His course. That is to say "be afraid of sin." We should resent sin because of its consequences.

The second kind of fear is the fear that is described as anxious concern that ends up in solitude. It causes us to dread the other person or thing. It brings to our mind all sorts of emotional terror, panic, fright, trepidation, horror, anger, hate, and dismay. This is the unwanted fear that besieges man in times of tragedy. It is this fear that makes us ask the question, **"Why me?"**

Fear that comes after a tragedy or as a result of distrust is of a very powerful but negative force. It brings about some strong negative emotions that cripple all good feelings. Sometimes it follows the surrounding events and responses from people around. Some people thrive on such fear by taking advantage of those who are already weakened by tragedy, thereby increasing their vulnerability to fear. Those who are afflicted must stay away from such people. These may be friends, family members, co-workers, neighbors, or even church members or anybody. The devil can attack us from anywhere. We must not succumb to his will. This is when you ask God to give you the wisdom to recognize these people and stay away from them.

"Your wisdom begins with total submission to Christ. When you begin to surrender completely, every part of you to His will, then you will begin to distance yourself from these enemies of progress" or the things of this world that cause you to fear and be without hope.

As you read this book, I want you to know and be able to tell others that fear is a negative feeling and can destroy its captive completely. It steals in like a thief, brings in other negative feelings, and holds its captive hostage. Fear is an emotional feeling that results from its own consequences. When we succumb to fear, we end up with the very things that we are afraid of.

As time passed by, I saw my weaknesses, and I decided to surround my family with God's armor. My friends were mostly fellow Christian and God-fearing people. I prayed strongly that God would bless me each day with those that I would find favor from and who would be blessed by my contact with them. God never fails. He heard my prayers and brought me in close contact with kind and loving people to comfort me.

I learned to **discipline myself to the fear of God.** It took me long to realize what I needed, but the good thing is that I was able to get there. I was able to see God's hand on me and I followed His directions. When children are involved in any kind of adversity, they too must be disciplined to the fear of God. No person is to be excluded. As I prayed for God to make me the best single parent that could be, I prayed also for Him to bless my children and make them my joy. They too needed to be disciplined for us to work together. Although I would give my children credit for good behavior, I must attribute it to the discipline they had from the beginning.

Fear has no room in our lives, especially when we call ourselves Christians. No child of God should settle for fear. We know very well that God did not give us any spirit of fear. We need to learn to go on in life as soldiers for Christ. For many months, I dwelt in negative things and thought that I had nothing to be happy for anymore in life. One thing that I did not give up was my prayer, but I did not care what I prayed, as long as I told God what was on my mind. Things were not easy. The nights were empty and dreamless. Little or no sleep came through my eyes. I kept on praying regardless. I knew that I was not getting the answers that I need from God. I spoke to some friends at my church and to most people in the same predicament as mine. As I continued to discipline myself with prayer and prayer groups, I began to realize that even though I am a Christian, I had not been praying right. I needed to pray with other people and also pray for other people (intercessory prayer). Trusting, hoping and praying with faith were not enough. One must also pray for other people and love them too.

It was through prayer meeting and talking to people about my worries that I found out about the weapon of the great enemy, FEAR. Satan will use fear to destroy God's children. Fear was my problem. Many ill or negative feelings may engulf us spiritually when we allow Satan to enter our hearts. Satan destroys man in any form possible. In sickness, death, or any form of affliction, we must not blame God or ask why He is making us suffer. God will do everything possible to make His children happy. If for any reason we have to blame anyone, it has to be the devil.

I have categorized these emotional feeling brought about by fear into three. Fear will cause **anger, guilt, and eventually lead us to failure.** We suffer these in our adversity or afflictions. If even you may have felt these emotions or may one day face such, know that you can easily overcome them just as I did. The word of God has helped me to stand strong in my life and you will receive the same strength if only you believe. We must be disciplined to know that fear and it's outcomes have no room where God's children are.

Fear will kill every hope, faith, love and peace any child of God has. We must not succumb to fear. Fear would lead us into anger and make us feel guilty of the very things we are afraid of. This eventually will cause failure. These are the devil's plan but we should never settle for what the devil has. I prayed about it, and I knew very well that God wants for us a life free from fear. The consequences of fear do not end with **anger, guilt, and failure** but will continue until the victim is helpless or even till death.

These and many more untold feelings are the plagues that face man when we let fear overtake us in times of adversity. Our fears and the result of our fears work together to make us or destroy us. Fear of man will prevent us from progressing, from worshiping God and even from living a fruitful life. We must cast away the fear of man and accept the fear of God to live fully as faithful Christians. You can pray all you want, but if you cannot discipline yourself from the fear of man, you will always be a slave to fear. Many Christians today suffer from fear, regardless of their life ordeal.

God has equipped us with wonderful scriptures from the Bible that give us words of wisdom and knowledge. We have inspirational song or hymns that give us comfort and consolations. We are fully equipped to defeat the devil and live on to glory.

I could not live any more days of my life in fear of anything man can do to me since I have known that God is with me all the way and that nothing could happen to me in my life that He could not handle for me. I just have to trust Him. Why then should I worry or be afraid of tomorrow? Why should I worry about how to raise my children? Why should I be afraid of what man would do? Is this not enough for me that God has promised me deliverance and protection? This same promise is for everyone who, whether in adversity or affliction, would wonder what God is doing to help him or her.

Anger:

Whenever there is adversity, affliction, or tribulation in our lives, we tend to first react in anger. **"Why me," is a strong reaction to anger and disappointment.** Years went by, and as I met more and more people with different problems, I realized that virtually everyone with one kind of problem or the other was angry at something or with someone, and more often with God or even at himself or herself. We all have one reason or the other to be angry for something. I found out that being angry would not help the fact that something bad had happened. The question is, how do we deal with it? It was hard to say or believe then that I must turn my eyes upon JESUS, but that was exactly what I needed to do without questions.

I now ask myself the question, "What right did I have to question God or be angry at Him?" I should not be angry with myself or anyone else either, because of things that I could not change or understand. As a matter of fact, why would anyone be angry with the same God that said that He would never leave us or forsake us?

The scriptures tells us in the book of Psalms 30:5:

"For his anger lasts only a moment, but his favor lasts a lifetime: weeping may remain for a night, but rejoicing comes in the morning."

God is love and will give us abundant love. He is not angry with me or with you. The comfort I received, knowing that weeping would only last but for a night and that there will be joy in the morning was part of what kept me going. I learned to have confident that each new day would bring a new hope. I was determined to have my hope only on Christ knowing that he alone is my strength.

According to God's word, we should refrain from anger and turn from wrath; do not fret—it leads only to evil **(Psalms 37:8).** We need to understand that no matter what our predicament may be, the first thing to learn is to refrain from anger. We cannot make things better or make any effective change when we are angry. We cannot pray effectively or faithfully in anger. My fears of the future made me not only feel unsafe with most people but also increased my anger towards them. Fear will precede anger, which becomes the beginning of other ill feelings such as hate, distrust, and discomfort. You cannot pray in anger and expect a faithful answer from God. I refrained from anger, learned through the help of other Christians to love myself. This was the beginning of my freedom, to love my children who I wanted so much to please, and my faithful friends and family members.

You should not hate those who have done you wrong or disappointed you at any time in life, especially during your affliction. Even when you reject them and distrust them or are angry with them or fear their relationship as much as you want to, the truth is that these negative responses to anger would always be nothing but discomfort to you. The enemy will always rejoice because he sets a trap for you through those who disappoint you and then watches you languish in your foolishness. I learned to pray for my enemies and those who despise me. Every Christian knows to do that, but sometimes we are carried away in our egoistic life and decide that we can handle things the way we would like to. I prayed for peace in my heart. Peace comes by asking God. I knew that God would give me peace, and I started to ask for peace. Through prayer, God granted me the peace that I needed to carry on with my life. I was able to trade my anger for peace. As I read the scripture every day, I began to realize that God's promises would only come through in my life if I did what He has asked me to do. Just praying was not enough. I had to put my prayer to practice. I must pray some real tough prayer and must do it with all my heart and stand by my prayers while doing my work.

The Scripture says in the book of Matthew, 5:44,
"But I say unto you, Love your enemies,
Bless them that curse you,
Do good to them that hate you and pray for
Them which despitefully use you, and persecute you."

It seems always like the scriptures do not make sense until we have a reason to justify those words. It never made sense that I should actually pray for my enemy until I realized the peace that comes with it. I asked God to deliver me from my enemies and protect me from them.

In verses 45-48, Christ tells us what God can do to both the good and the evil ones, and that we have no reward from God if we love only those who love us. If we would love and pray for our enemies, we would be free from blame and from their evil plans. Do not be afraid to pray for your enemies. The enemy is Satan and he puts fear in you to destroy you, but the greatest weapon you have to fight the enemy is honest and faithful prayer added with total surrender of yourself to Christ. This would give you power and make you strong daily. You will surprise all those who despise and hate you because your strength is renewed daily as you pray. You would be able to stand strong and upright before your enemies in the end.

Guilt:

We should not let the guilt that follows adversity prevent us from seeing the good things God has promised His children. Guilt is a feeling of responsibility for wrongdoing. Sometimes we tend to accept guilt, even when it is not due. In times of trouble, we tend to find reasons to blame someone or even blame ourselves for things we feel we could have done but did not. We make excuses for everything, as long as it will justify our behavior at that time. Most people who are afflicted tend to accept the guilty feeling imposed on them by the devil, which I call the enemy of progress. You must not let the devil deceive you or stop you from moving on in life.

In sickness, we make excuses to justify why or why not we should be sick. In death, we find reasons why or why not it should have happened. Sometimes people try to justify things by their own feelings, and may even pass judgment on others right away. A young man felt guilty for being the driver of a car that was involved in a fatal accident. A lady felt guilty for not standing strong to reprimand her husband about his drinking habit until he died in a car crash. He had been drinking and decided to drive home at a late hour. A mother blames herself for a child who chose to live an unworthy life. In times of tragedy, guilty feelings can weigh us down and lead to serious emotional breakdown. I oftentimes wonder if there was anything I could have done to bring my beloved husband or my sister back to life. These were people who died at the times I needed them most in my life. I felt like my profession should have helped me to understand that they were going to die. I felt like everything that could have stopped these deaths eluded me.

If I was not sleeping, could I have stopped him from dying? Maybe I did not scream hard enough to call him back to life. Why did I not notice something wrong? Why did he not give me a sign or a hint? Did God let him die just to punish me? What of my sister, what could I have done? Does it mean that I did not pray hard enough? Guilt will bring us to shame, cause sadness, and leave us with loneliness. It was very hard for me to comprehend something that I could not explain, nor have any clue as to how it works, and that is the deaths of my loved ones. I lived in the bondage of guilt until I learned that nothing was in my hands and that I could not have done anything to change or stop these things.

I found many people in the same situation. Instead of looking up to God for help and praying for guidance, most people in this predicament would sit and waste in fear and guilt.

From the book of 1 John 3:20:

Whenever our hearts condemn us, we should turn to God who is greater than our hearts and knows everything. We need not be afraid. We need not let the guilt brought by fear be a hindrance to our joy. Guilt would make you hide and feel downcast. This brings about loneliness, sadness and shame.

One of the major reasons for the feeling of shame in times of adversity or afflictions is the lack of trust in God and the fear of failure. I was afraid of what will happen next. I held onto my affliction as the reason for my negative emotions. It did not help at all. All I needed was to turn to God through Christ. I waited and worried too long before I realized what to do.

Romans 10:11, "For the scripture saith, whosoever believeth on him shall not be ashamed."

If we believe in God, we have no reason to let anything put us to shame.

Loneliness creeps in when we are afraid. I found out that with many people, their fear started from the moment they started thinking, "How could I do it or how could I survive it?" Many people are afraid of being alone in times of sickness, death, traveling, and most of all in their daily living. Those who lose their loved ones are afraid of being alone. Some are afraid of carrying on with life's responsibilities. It is absolutely impossible for this category of people to live alone and so they need another figure to replace their loss or at least come close to replacing that loss. Why should we be lonely when we know that God is with us. He tells us in the book of **John 14:18** that he will not leave us as orphans. When you feel like you are alone, call on God, He would not stay away from you. According to His many promises, He would never forsake you nor leave you. You will call and the Lord will answer; you will cry for help, and He will say: Here am I **(Isaiah, 58:9)**. There shall be no fear or loneliness when we are with God. Surrendering our thoughts, fears, and worries to Him delivers us from our sorrows.

Failure

Forgiveness comes as a result of discipline. Those who are disciplined by the love of God, will often times find it easy to forgive. People find it difficult to confess their sins. Those who offend their brothers must ask for forgiveness. But there are people who under no circumstance would agree to confess and ask for forgiveness. In our daily lives, or even in adversity, we run into people who are very adamant about their ego. They would not ask for forgiveness. When we look at the consequences of not forgiving people, it becomes realistic that no matter what may betide, you must forgive such people just for your own good. This was a lesson that I learned as I asked God to direct my life. I must forgive my enemies in every circumstance because that was the only way my burden, which is laid before Christ, would be lifted from me. When you forgive people, even though you may not see them, you pray for them that it will be well with them. They might refuse to confess and ask for forgiveness, but that would be between them and God not you. As a Christian, if you would pray for such people, you would free your heart from the aches and pains of unforgiving, which also brings about failure. We must be disciplined to forgive people who hurt our feelings especially in times of adversity.

I needed favor from God and I knew I had to ask with a clean heart, so I had to truly forgive my debtor, no matter where they were. I would not be who I am or where I am today if I had not learned to forgive those who despise and forsake me. When you realize that only God has power over your life, you will stand strong in Him and put all enemies behind you. Then you will surprise them. **Only through Christ can I do all things, because he strengthens me.** Unforgiving can destroy our health as it lowers our immune system. It can cause poverty and lead to defeat. To fail is to become unsuccessful, fall short, or become inadequate. No one wants to fail or be found inadequate. I was buried in thoughts as well as in works. I worried about failure so much that I could not focus on Christ. My feelings were not in any form different from the feelings of most other people, men and women that I came in contact with. I did not want to fail in my duty as a parent. I did not want my children to fail in their duties at home, or in their school and in the community. Fear of failure may be of different categories. It may be the fear of failure to provide adequate care such as food, personal time, and love for the home. It may be failure to stand strong against your adversaries. I was found in all of these and more.

Was it possible to let go? How could I forgive or forget death or whatever was responsible for my loss? I sought ways to recoil in my very little shell and just shut off every irritable thing or person. The more I tried, the more memories came back to mind. Crying sometimes seemed to be the best thing to do. I would crawl up in my bed and weep through the night. **God alone understands the tears of a widow, the questions in the eyes of an orphan, and the prayers of the afflicted.** Those that you comforted and stretched your hands to help when they needed your help may decide to despise you when you are afflicted. You may be dropped from a high-rank, hard-working, kind and cheerful giver to be called a failure. When your faith in God and your patience are tried, even by those you least expected would do so, you are supposed to be strong. Continue to look up to God. It took me time to realize what I was going through. Through the help of other Christians, I learned to pray for these people. I asked God to lead me so that I will not fail. He answered my prayers. My life was changed and God's blessings were showered on me.

Most Christians walk around blind in their own little faith, thinking that they could see. I was one of them. When you develop a relationship with your Heavenly Father and start to pray right, you would know what it means to forgive your worst enemy, and you will see a difference (God's miracle) in your life. **We take God's kindness for granted and we neglect His words.** I knew His promises to man and all He has promised me as a widow. I claimed these promises. Praying for my enemies and being able to know that I have truly forgiven them was one good thing that happened to me as a result of my association with other Christians. I met with several single parents and very successful people. Each person at one time or the other had felt like I did. I had the opportunity to attend several women's retreats with most women from my church, and each time I learned something new to help strengthen my Christian belief. One of my most rewarding experiences was to know the joy of freedom from hate. It is a great thing to stop everything and pray for your enemy. As you read on in this book, you will find out why I am telling you right now that you must forgive those who wrong you, especially those that took your kindness for granted. It hurts to be wronged but do not wait and ponder like I did. Start now to pray. The Lord blessed me, He will bless you too.

We Christians tend to hold onto our anger for so long, yet claiming that we have faith in God. We will never find out what good we are missing from the love of Christ when we continue to hold onto our anger. As I said earlier, I could not enjoy the peace and joy from our Father in heaven until I learned to let go. Understanding the word of God changed my lifestyle, my prayer pattern, and the way I perceived things. For those who are asking and wanting to know my secret, I would say that knowing God, and being honest and persistent in my prayers and daily duty was a great tool in raising my children and doing all that I found myself doing.

Several texts in the Bible tell us about forgiveness and what God wants of us. I was touched by a few of these scriptures. No one but God would know how I felt, realizing that I have to endure my pains and try to live like everything was all right. I knew that it was not going to be easy. God wants us to forgive and we must do it. What will be the consequences of not trying to retaliate? Why would someone else be happy and not me? Why will I allow someone to hurt my feelings and get away with it? What would I gain by forgiving? Does it mean that my enemy is then free and I am left to suffer my pains?

These thoughts and more plagued my mind. As I searched the Bible, I began to see the answers to every one of these questions clearly. The scriptures tell us:

Mathew 5:44-45

"...and pray for them which despitefully use you, and persecute you;

That ye may be children of your Father, which is in heaven: for he maketh his sun to rise on the evil and on the good, and sendeth rain on the just and on the unjust."

If we pray for our enemies, the Bible tells us that we would be called the children of God. Because He cares for both the good and the bad, we should pray and allow Him to take care of both the good and the bad, our joys and our problems. **Mathew 6:14** also tells us that if we forgive our enemies, our Heavenly Father would also forgive us our sins. It is therefore important that we should listen to the word of God. Since we know that all have sinned and have come short of God's glory, we know that we are all sinners and if we forgive our debtors, God will forgive us our debts. When I started to forgive people, regardless of who they were or what they did to me, I began to receive the spirit of peace and joy in me. I knew that I would be a winner and that God would surely protect me from those enemies. God does not only forgive you your sins, but He also blesses you. At this point in my life, I would not dare harbor any grudge in my heart for anyone. This is not to say that I would not stand against evildoers; rather I mean that no evil planned by any man would separate me from my Savior. I have found my peace in knowing Him.

God does not want us to pay back evil for evil. We must understand this. If you cannot reach your enemies, be sure to pray for them. Because we know that there is evil and that the devil hangs around preying on God's children, we must pray constantly without ceasing for both the devil, the enemy we know or see, and the one we could not see or reach.

Proverbs 20:22—"Say not thou, I will recompense evil; but wait on the Lord, and he shall save you."

It takes a lot of discipline to pray rightly for your enemy. It is not easy to tell someone to love and pray for their enemies, let alone saying, *Do not retaliate, be kind and merciful to them.* You have to accept them if they would come; and give them if they should ask of you. This was quite an experience. It was not easy to pray for my foes, but I did it with all my heart and God heard my prayers and blessed me. I sincerely pray for their success because I believe that if their lives would be satisfactory to them, they would be happy where they are, and I would be free of their trouble. It sounds unchristian to say be happy where

147

you are so that I will be happy with myself. But this is a true prayer if you should come to reality. No matter how much forgiveness you accord some people, they would surely bring you back to the slum. I prayed to God to help them and free me from their bondage. God wants us to pray for our enemies…pray for their good. Be kind to your enemies. Do not give them evil which is what they have given you, especially if they should ask.

In the book of **Luke 6:38**, the scripture says that we should give and it will be given to us. …

"For with the measure you use, it will be measured to you." If you would want the good measure, pressed down, shaken together, and running over, then you should give the same and watch God pour His blessing on you. Forgiveness is what God requires of us. It will be a blessing to us according to His promises to man. But when we refuse to forgive, the repercussion is, by far, more than we could imagine, we will be walking towards failure in life.

Unforgiving attitude, even on those who have deliberately hurt us, has a tremendous setback on people's lives. It can cause failure, sickness, and even poverty. These are the things we dread most, especially in time of adversity or affliction. When I spoke to different people who suffer some kind of hurt in their hearts, especially those who lost their loved ones, I realized that in most cases, these people are hurting because of a feeling or a grudge over something or someone in relation to their loss. Some may be angry at the sickness or disease that affected their loved ones. Some may be angry with someone who did not respond to their feelings at their time of hurt. Some may even be angry at themselves or the caregiver before death, or even at God for not intervening in their favor. These feelings could cause more pain than the actual problems especially when we allow them to rule our lives.

I was determined to look at the best examples and be the best. I knew that most widows and other people have passed through all kinds of life's storms and still rejoiced in the Lord. I equally knew that there were many more looking for a way out from their ordeal. If there is the best, I was determined to be part of it. By the same token, there are men or even children who have lost their loved ones and therefore have given up hope in life, saying, "It is not fair, life is not fair." I was determined not to give up. I knew my God and I knew that He would not leave me to stand alone. I am saying to those people today that **God has not given you a spirit of fear, but of power, and of love, and of sound mind (2 Timothy 1:7).** You should therefore not be ashamed of the testimony of our Lord. You should not claim failure.

In the beginning of this book, we read that every person on the surface of this earth is created for a purpose. Sometimes it is hard to find what God wants you to do. Some people live their entire life on earth and die not knowing why they were here. The Bible tells us that whatever your hands find to do, you should do it with all your might. I asked God for strength, and peace of mind, that I may forgive and forget my hurt. I wanted to be my best to my family. I will go down to the basics, which is to put God first in my life and let Him direct my ways. All I wanted was for Him to direct me. When you ask and God answers, there should be no going back. **It was not easy for me. I prayed and cried constantly because of the lifestyle that I wanted to live. I know that it was not going to be easy at all. I must make a sacrifice if I want to be true to myself.** But I knew that in my spiritual life, my God was first. I must satisfy my Maker so as to take care of my children. I would have to forgive, forget, be nice, be kind, be strong, believe, trust, have faith, and so on to have a sound mind. The greatest was to give my life to God through Christ my Savior. I thought that I was already a Christian and that was all there was in knowing God. No, we must be faithful and obedient to God. I was afraid that I would not have a life if I did all that I had to do to be faithful to God. When I realized that I must take an extra step in life for my faith, I asked God to give me a final answer to my prayers.

One Sabbath morning, I left my children at home and went to church very early. I knew that the–prayer group usually starts at about 8 o'clock in the morning. I did not want to ask to have the church doors open early for me, so I waited till about 8 o'clock. I only came to pray and tell God something. I was lucky to see that the prayer group at that time was only about three people sitting in a corner at the overflow area of the church. I walked towards the pulpit and with a little room for privacy, I was comfortable to tell God my needs. I knelt down and sobbed bitterly. **"Lord, take me now in your hands and use me for whatever purpose. Take me, and my children and use us as you would. My life is in your hands, from today. Father, I know you have a plan for which you created me. Take away my fears and discouragement, and show me that purpose. Surround me with positive influences so that I would make a difference for you in my life especially in my children and those that may come my way."** I prayed for about thirty minutes and when I got up, I noticed that a few more people had come in to church. I realized that one of the older ladies was watching me. I looked at her and smiled and she said something like, "God bless you." I left and went home. Shortly after, I returned to church with my children.

While I was praying, I had a feeling of gloom and darkness. My heart was heavy, but right before I stopped, I felt like a hand had touched me and someone said, **"Stop crying, I will be with you, I will be your husband and your children are my children. If you believe, it will**

be well with you." I thought that someone had put some ice water on me. I stopped praying, opened my eyes, and gradually rose up and wiped off my eyes. There was no one near me. As I left the church, my heart felt free from a heavy burden. I felt like I had told God everything and knew that He would answer my prayers. Things had been very rough. But I knew that God had made me a promise and I must claim it both mentally and spiritually. This happened at the time that I was mourning my older sister's death and I had been called to join a newly-formed women's group in my community as a patron of the association. When they asked me what name would I like to be known as, I did not have any name to give. It was a custom for the members and female patrons to have a nickname or another name of interest that they would like to be called. A few people suggested all kinds of names that pleased their feeling of me but I knew that my spirit would not accept such names. After some strong prayers, God revealed a name to me: **Nwanyichinalu**, meaning "woman married by God." Yes, Chinalum, meaning "God is my husband." That became my name, and ever since I claimed God's promises, He has not forsaken me nor left me alone. **If you would also believe in Him, it will be well with you.** That was the statement He made to me when He comforted me. God is wonderful and good in all our lives.

I asked God to show me my duty in life, especially with my family. I have no physical spouse. I want you to show the world that you are not just the husband to the widow but that you are equally the father to the fatherless. Tell the world that you are my husband and the father of my children. I found out that all God wanted from me was for me to open my mouth and ask with all my heart. In any situation in your life, do praise God. He is the only one that could change and direct your ways. He would not do it alone, just like He would not let you do it alone. God needs you to work with

Him. I gave my life to Him so that He could direct me, I learned to work with Him through prayer and amazingly, He has blessed me.

In the month of October 1996, I had the opportunity to go to a women's retreat with my church family. Camp Cedar Falls is a popular retreat center for the Seventh Day Adventists in Southern California. My family is very familiar with the camp, since we had been there several times before for the Redondo Beach church family retreats. At this time, it was a women's retreat. Years ago I remember waking up early every morning, sneaking out of our cabin to go and run up and down the hills before every other camper woke up. I had been awake all night, thinking and visualizing how Elijah, Moses, Abraham, and all the men of the Bible built their trust in God. I could visualize the prayers by the brooks and rivers of the Bible cities. I could hear them as they laid their sacrifices and request in the valleys and on the hills and mountains. I could recall all the Bible stories we heard as children and tried to visualize them as an adult. Although these were men and my needs might not be same as theirs, my heart also yearned for God's protection and deliverance as theirs did. I made up my mind that I must talk to God as they did. In the wee hours of the cold mountain air, I rose from my bed in search of what I now call **the advent of my new hope.**

The fog was thick in this mountain area. The dew had gotten heavy through the night. The morning was chilly. There was no single sound or sense of life around. No bird whistling and no wind of course. I was determined and steadfast in my quest to talk to God alone. I had just ventured to run up the hill when I realized that it had been some years since I did that last. I slowed down and carefully walked up the hill. There was no sound or anyone else around. That was what I needed, a quiet time with God alone. As I walked up higher and higher, I started reciting **"the Lord is my**

shepherd, (Psalm 23)... I shall not want..." He cares for me. Even though I walk through the valley of the shadow of death, I shall not fear any evil. God is with me.

He will comfort me and uplift me, even before my enemies. How wonderful to know that I will live in His house forever. Slowly and steadily, I walked up the hill, as I listened to my voice now singing the 23rd Psalm. It was cool and quiet and I walked and walked until I came to a comfortable point, high and secluded enough for the privacy I needed. I looked around for a better spot should someone else decide to seek God like I was, but there was no spot better than where God had planted my feet.

I knelt down and said, in preparation to pray, "Dear Heavenly Father, I...." As though someone pulled me up hard, suddenly I sprang up on my feet. I thought that I had started wrong. Standing and looking straight to the top of the mountains, I felt the chill of the mountain air, fresh and cold. With my two hands straight down at my sides, my fists tightly clenched, and my shoulders shrugged, I tightened my face as I fought tears, hot tears rolling down my cheek. My tears prepared me for my prayer. I was relaxed after a few tears. I raised my hand to the mountain and said, *"Lord, as I face the rising sun, on this hill will I lay down my burden again to you. Tell me what to do to be saved and teach me to do right and teach my children right. You know my problems. I want to make a difference in raising my children. I do not want to suffer the setbacks from this society. Teach me to teach my children right. I want us to walk in your light. Bless and bless us abundantly and teach us to bless others with what you have blessed us with. Finally, Lord if I have to bear this burden, teach me how, walk and work with me. According to your promises, never leave us alone.*

This was the second time I was touched by my close walk with God. It was another faithful prayer and the beginning of a strong hope in Christ. At the end of my prayer, I sat on the sand and I saw myself talking to my Heavenly Father like we were having a great conversation over what we prayed about. Shortly after, people started waking up and coming uphill for their morning walk. I went back to my cabin with a heart full of joy and hope for better life.

CHAPTER NINE

How Shall I Look Back?

I have learned that if I should ever look back, it has to be with hope, having come so close to accomplishing my goals. Some may call us lucky, some may call us blessed. Regardless of what you may choose to say, I must say that the best part of my journey is that when I look back, I see that my hope in God through Christ my Savior is still strong and was never in vain. There were difficult times. Those times that I would have to plan and make decisions, knowing that I could not please one child and forget the others. Times when I had to budget for one child, realizing that the other ones are waiting for their turns. Times when I had to discipline myself in order to discipline my child. Times when I felt like screaming my head off but could not, for fear of misrepresentation. Times when I had to scream anyway, regardless of the consequence, I had to spare the child and break the rod. In looking back, I know that I must not forget how we got to where we are now. If not for God's grace, **it could have been worse.** As I look back, I want to continuously thank God for His grace and love.

When we have life, we must have hope. Our expectations in life make our hope in life. I asked God to fulfill my hope, I trusted Him and prayed faithfully, and He answered my prayers. I asked for His will and He allowed me to know what He wants me to do. It is my sincere heart's desire to do His will. I love to use the saying that: **"When the master is glorified, the servant is satisfied."** The pains and the hurts of adversities and afflictions may be laid in your heart. It is up to you to keep these with you or put them aside or trade them with the wonderful promises of God.

His grace, His love and His ever-presence…. never leaving me or forsaking me, is sufficient for me. I must therefore glorify Him.

This book simplifies my journey through adversity. Some men or women may have been scorned or battered. Some may have suffered some sort of abuse or other, even from loved ones or trusted family members. Some may have lost a loved one such as a child, spouse, friend, parents, or even neighbors. Some may have been jailed for crimes they did not commit. It may be poverty, lack of respect, ill health, or society complex. It could be anything, from being refused a piece of bread to the denial of a long-expected promotion at a workplace. You may have worked hard to confidently say to yourself, "I am sure that everything is fine now." But tragedy hits and every hope seems lost. As you read this, you are taking this journey with me. I pray that it will help you to realize how much God loves you. The songs and Bible verses and many more have been laid down for us as a token of love from our Heavenly Father. When we see and read His words and keep His commands, then we would have opened up a relationship with Him.

This relationship is our goal to success. I found my consolation when I realized that God had equipped me and even you with everything needed to survive and succeed in life.

My children were never my problem, as I had thought. I wanted to raise them right. Out of fear and anxiety, I thought that I could not do that duty. I asked questions and I had doubts. But when I turned to God in faithful prayers and honestly and totally surrendered my life to Him, I found my refuge, in Him through Christ. He delivered me, blessed my family and told me that I should bless other people with His blessings on me. I can strongly say now that, **those whom God has blessed, or whatever God has destined, no man can change. It is written and so it is."**

156

You now can see how I did it. Everything that looks good is not always easy. When we trust in God, things start looking easy, even though the devil will find a way to make things hard. The things I asked for, God provided. The things I hoped for, He fulfilled for me. I have no reason not to praise Him with one of my favorite songs:

Great is thy faithfulness, O God my father
There is no shadow of turning with thee
Thou changest not, thy compassions they fail not
As thou hast been thou forever wilt be
Great is thy faithfulness! Great is thy faithfulness!
Morning by morning new mercies I see
*All I have needed thy hand hath provided
*Great is thy faithfulness, Lord unto me!

For every man or woman who at this moment is going through any form of adversity, I want you all to know that you are not alone. God is not only watching and caring for you, He has also provided for you in all areas of life. He is only waiting for you to claim His promises for you so that you may live and be happy. God surrounds you with His people. Look up, step out, and say something to someone, and you will be surprised to know that He has given you people for your physical help. Pray to Him and you will see His angels doing marvelous things for you and giving you spiritual uplifting. Believe in Him and you will hear His voice answering you when you call. Praise Him at all times and in everything. Remember that whatever problem you have, it could have been worse if not for His grace. Sing songs of praise to God. Thank Him every day for your life. Ask for wisdom in all your decisions. Be happy for somebody else's life, love them, love yourself, but most of all, love God your Heavenly Father and delight yourself in His ways.

When we pray to God for help, we must also remember that He does not want to leave us alone. He wants to work with us. Any prayer without work is a dead prayer. So we must work with God as we pray to Him. Be willing to listen to Him and do your part of the work. Your children will grow with what they see. If you choose and do right, most likely they would choose and do right and your dreams would be fulfilled.

As a parent, you must make sure that you lay a good foundation of trust with your children. (This is something I would like to discuss in my next book.) All parents, especially single parents, must learn to do what they say or say what they do. When we start regretting over our children's behavior, we must first look back at ourselves before we look at the society. Who comes first, parents or society?

You ask me how I did it? I would say to you again that it was all by the grace of God through prayer and supplications, then persistent hard work. I found a great gift of life from God as I walked and worked with Him during my times of grief. It was the gift of patience. I realized that God has so much patience for us and wants us to be patient too in order to receive His answers to our prayers. In answering my prayers, God opened my eyes to see His abundant love and care for me. He wiped away my tears and showed me my duty to Him. **God revealed to me that if I should worry about anything or anybody, it should be all those who are lost in hope;** the many children all over the world who have lost every hope for better life. There are orphans, and those children who are stricken with poverty, especially in the poorer, so-called third world countries. God wants you and me to worry and care about such people. God blesses us so that we would be a blessing to others. When God hears and answers your prayers, He wants you to be a blessing to someone else too. You can do this by witnessing for Him or by giving a helping hand to others.

It has been my desire to give back to God as He has been giving me. Three years after I started my deeper walk with my Heavenly Father, I began to see His hand work on my family. Even as a woman of little faith, I still doubted what He had in store for me. I did not stop fasting and praying. Thanks to the women ministry and prayer warriors in my church, I was blessed with spirit-filled women. These sisters, by faith, helped me to learn how to fast and pray. Through the ministry, I learned that I was not and will never be alone. I learned that the grass was not really greener in my neighbor's yard. I must keep praying until something good happens.

My husband and I lived our lives with the passion to help others. After he passed away, I realized that people were not real when it came to adversity. You are judged quickly by those you trust and even those you cared for most. When, in their judgment, they think that you would not be able to stand on your own or as before, they quickly find reasons to desert you. Because of such people, I started to withdraw from what I knew and did very well which was to give a helping hand to the needy. God threw me in among these women of grace who prayed for me and with me. They helped me to retrace my steps and be who God had already said that I would be. I remember once, following one of those sad events when you would sit and wonder why some people are the way they are, when my little child saw me so sad, she made a statement that taught me a great lesson, saying, "Mommy, it is time for you to start helping the needy and not the greedy." This child was right. Her statement gave me food for thought. There are people who need help and there are some who want help. We must chose right because in the end, only what was done for Christ would count.

In 1997, seeing the events in my Nigerian-American community, I decided to call some of my friends together to form a support group for our fast-growing families and our children. The response was overwhelming. **NMADINOBI,** meaning **BEAUTY IS IN THE HEART,** was soon adopted as the name for the group. This is a non-profit support group that has grown beyond serving our children and families and now is reaching out to other areas in the county of Los Angeles. Part of the goals and objectives of this association is to help and support the needy, the afflicted, the homeless, and the sick by visiting **homeless shelters, nursing homes, and needy families.** Our visitations include, but are not limited to, donation of food and/or money, serving food, and more importantly, spiritual uplifting of the individuals involved. As the founder of this group, I have grown to appreciate the love of God and the work He has done in the members since the inception. Our membership is based on finding some mature Igbo women who are willing to serve other people who are underprivileged, not only with all their hearts but with love and passion.

In my quest to continue to serve God's children, I have adopted a motherless children's home (orphanage) in my hometown. In the same city, I have extended a helping hand with scholarships to some underprivileged young men and women in their education and daily survival, especially the orphans and widows of WIN (Widows in Need) Group. At this moment, I have jointly registered and started a non-profit rescue home with other faithful believers in the city of Lagos, Nigeria for all people and of all walks and faith. No one is limited from getting God's blessings from this home. I pray that God will direct those who need help to be reached through this ministry. **GOLD CREST FAMILY CENTER (Potters House)** is already in operation.

It is my vision to see other people blessed by the blessings God has given me. He has given me the joy of peace and love. He has given me joy of knowing Him and recognizing that He is my Heavenly Father. He has taken away my fears. He healed my wounds and cleansed me. He fed me when I was hungry. He wiped away my tears. He comforted me and blessed me indeed. Even though I walk through the valley of the shadow of death, I will fear no evil because He is with me.

I want you to believe and He will always do for you according to His promises. No matter what may come your way, I want you to know that God will never leave you to suffer. I was afraid of how I could take care of my children without my husband. God showed me a way and told me that He will bless me and enlarge my territory enough and I would be able to care for more than just my children. With Him, all things are possible.

In looking back, I must say that I am amazed by God's love. I will live to praise His name. I cannot tell enough of God's blessings on me. As a pharmacist and a naturopath, being a single parent and trying to keep up with life has not been easy for me. As a business owner, I have equally worked several twenty-four hour days. As a widow, I have had several sleepless nights. As a Christian, I have had countless moments of doubt and fears, while holding onto my faith. I am still taking this journey, except that right now, I have completely surrendered all to God through Christ who is my strength and redeemer. Being able to love myself has helped me to love my children, fellow people, even my enemies, and most importantly my Maker. By so doing I have claimed His promises and love and that is why most of you would see me and say, "You are blessed."

CONCLUSION

It is important for everyone to know that you cannot claim God's promises just by saying "I believe in God." In **Matthews 7:21**, Christ tells us that it is not all who say to him, "Lord, Lord" that will enter the kingdom of Heaven, but he that doeth the will of my father in heaven. A closer relationship with God comes through prayer. As the author and finisher of our lives, we must not take His Grace (favors) on us for granted. If we claim His grace and promises, we must then not mourn like we are void of hope. Our daily lives must reflect His love on us. We must let our light (the love of Christ in us) shine so men would glorify Him.

Many people have survived difficult times. Many widows have made great single parents. Many who were afflicted have shown great faith. Many more will do greater and marvelous things. So when your storm of life comes, remember that you are not alone. You are not the first nor would you be the last. Cast away self pity and be prepared to walk and work with your Heavenly Father. Sing a joyful song. Pray a faithful prayer and surrender all about you to God. You will be amazed at what you can accomplish when God is on your side. Your enemies will bow down before you.

You may be able to sing my song of faith and trust saying:

"Yes God is good , in earth and sky."

We must now know that God does not create adversities. He actually prevents us from suffering the effects of our adversities. Adversities are not designed to destroy us rather our faith is supposed to be made stronger in times like these. We should not allow the calamities of this earth deprive us of the love of God. He will always bless us even in our times of storm if only we would trust Him and have faith in Him.

To every thing there is a season, and a time to every purpose under the haven, **Ecclesiastes 3:1**

So every joy or sorrow comes in its season. For those things we have no control over, we must completely surrender them to God. He is our able help in times of trouble.

In Prayer:

You are never alone. Listen to the voice of God. He hears you and wants you to hear Him too.

In humbleness and with confidence, present your need and question not His Powers.

Be faithful with strong hope, trusting that He will answer your prayers.

Pray for your family, which includes your children, spouse and yourself.

Pray for all other people including those who despise you.

Be thankful and give God Glory as you pray.

In Relationship:

Show love and be honest to God, other people and yourself.

Allow God to order your steps and guide you in your relationships.

Be a role model, teaching your children right and showing good examples.

Recognize the feelings of others especially of family and those around you.

Be a positive thinker and do not mingle or argue with unbelievers.

Be a blessing to those you come across and you will find favor in them.

In Service:

Give your best and serve with all of your heart when asked.

Be willing to share or give a helping hand to the poor or needy.

Visit the sick and the afflicted and give a word of encouragement.

Be patient and listen especially to the complaints of the afflicted.

Be responsible for what you do and ask God to bless your work.

Be careful, watchful and of all things be a faithful servant.

This may seem like a load of responsibilities, but actually it only means that you have to start living right. It is just a few of the guidelines for successful living. Try this and see if God will not bless you, and even your children will call you blessed.

Dear friends and readers, I ask you to take this journey with me. It is a journey of trust and faith. As you read this book, tell your friends about it. Your journey has become. It is a journey with our Heavenly Father. When you don't see His footprint, and life seems like a roller coaster, be still and know that He has just lifted you in His arms. So when you ask me how did I do it, I would gladly answer that it was through **prayer, holding onto my faith, and placing my hope and trust in God through Christ my Savior.**

Proceeds from this book will be used in part to support not only the poor and needy but also the many children found in those motherless homes where sometimes, they may fail to be adopted.

Remember, when you give, you give to the Lord. You too will be blessed.

DEDICATION

I would like to dedicate this book to my family, my children who gave me the reason and hope to keep praying every day. Also to my late husband Dr. Godfrey Asomugha, who was a loving and kind hearted husband and father. He laid the inspirational foundation upon which we stood to weather the storm of life. To my late sister, Peace Okwuadigbo, a woman of grace, who lovingly became my spiritual mentor from childhood. Finally to those who are weary and slumbering in faith, may God guide you and shine His light in your path that you may see and glorify His name.

ABOUT THE AUTHOR

Dr. Lilian Ijeoma Asomugha who now resides in Southern California is a dedicated Christian mother of four children. She strongly believes in the trademark of Christianity: Love and Truth. She is one of twelve children born to her parents in Eastern Nigeria where she was equally raised in the Christian faith.

In 1972 she was married to a handsome young man, Godfrey Asomugha who soon after their marriage left for United States of America to further his education. In 1974 while in Nigeria, she graduated from college and later joined her husband in the USA. She describes their reunion as a dream come true. Like most other immigrants, they had high hopes for the American dream.

While her husband studied Petroleum engineering, Lilian went back to school and studied Pharmacy and Naturopathic medicine. Their love for family, education and faith in God helped them to achieve their educational goals, and started to build a happy home.

As fate would have it, her husband, Dr. Godfrey Asomugha suddenly passed away in 1994 following a massive heart attack. "I was left to weather the storm of life alone", she says.

Her love for her children and her dedication to helping others reach their goals in life is her source of strength and the joy of her life. She has worked and served in the pharmaceutical industry for nearly three decades and uses the opportunity her profession affords her in reaching out to people especially the afflicted. Because of her willingness to give, she has often times been described as "The Philanthropist lady", helping and supporting those who are underprivileged.

Friends and family call her *"Nwanyichinalu"*, meaning, woman married by God. She is a prayer warrior and a persevering hard working mother who would stop at nothing to achieve any God given vision.

In her busy schedule, she finds time in interacting with people, motivating and counseling whenever she could. Her interests and hubby include, reading, writing, singing and planting (gardening).

Her interest in writing is based on her personal experiences, which she intends to use to motivate, inspire and uplift her readers. *The Advent of a New Hope* is her first book. She plans to write so be prepared to read from her.

LaVergne, TN USA
31 August 2010
195331LV00001B/8/A